There are some books that are not just needed, they are in fact necessary, and this book by my friend and brother Dr. Rolland Daniels is one of those necessary books.

There is no doubt but that we are living in challenging days and times, and one of the traits of the times is an absence and loss of civility. That has cost us more than we can fully evaluate or estimate.

In this book, Daniels recounts lessons, truths, parables, indeed "Habeyisms" that he learned from his dad. These lessons are as true now as when they were first told, and they are as needed now as ever.

If we are to recover who we are meant to be and live as we were made to live, then what Rolland's dad taught him—these principles, precepts, and practices—must be lessons we learn and live out in our lives as well. After all, that is how a legacy is made.

Read this book and be challenged and changed...

Timothy J. Clarke, Senior Pastor
First Church of God
Columbus, Ohio

Rolland Daniels is one of the most respected leaders in the Church of God, both here in the USA and around the globe. He has led some of our largest congregations, overseen the development of outreach tools for thousands of congregations, and encouraged pastors coast-to-coast. He has done this with a constant demeanor of enthusiasm and grace. I've admired him since I first met him while I was a student at Anderson University and he a student in the Anderson University Seminary. I had the privilege of knowing his brother, his parents, and some of the extended family. The love for the local church runs deep in this family. The character qualities described in this book were learned at the deep well of this "legacy" family.

As you read the pages of this book, you will be inspired to love others as Rolland has loved those around him. This book will feed your soul. It will call you into accountability. It will be a resource to share with others. It will serve as curriculum for Bible studies and, more than likely, a few Sunday messages along the way.

So grab a cup of coffee, sit in a comfortable chair, have a highlighter handy, and enjoy this inspiring book.

Marty Grubbs, Senior Pastor
Crossings Church
Oklahoma City, Oklahoma

legacy MAKER

LIVE A LIFE THAT MATTERS

ROLLAND E. DANIELS

LEGACY MAKER
LIVE A LIFE THAT MATTERS

iUniverse books may be ordered through booksellers or by contacting:

iUniverse
1663 Liberty Drive
Bloomington, IN 47403
www.iuniverse.com
1-800-Authors (1-800-288-4677)

The New International Version is an English translation of the Bible first published in 1978 by Biblica. The NIV was published to meet the need for a modern translation done by Bible scholars using the earliest, highest quality manuscripts available.

The New Living Translation is a translation of the Bible into modern English. Originally starting out as an effort to revise The Living Bible, the project evolved into a new English translation from Hebrew and Greek texts.

Holy Bible: New Living Translation. Wheaton, Ill: Tyndale House Publishers, 2004. Print. The New Life Version of the Bible is a simplified English translation by Gleason and Kathryn Ledyard.

ISBN: 978-1-5320-9638-9 (sc)
ISBN: 978-1-5320-9616-7 (hc)
ISBN: 978-1-5320-9639-6 (e)

Library of Congress Control Number: 2020905641

Cover photo by Shutterstock.com and cover design by Mary J. Jaracz Design.

Print information available on the last page.

iUniverse rev. date: 05/01/2020

Dedicated to my father, Everett L. Daniels: the finest man I ever knew, the greatest hero a son could have and the wisest man I ever learned from. Thanks, Dad, for all you were and all you meant to me.

Special thanks to Joe Allison and his team for truly making this book possible. Joe, I could not and would not have wanted to publish this book without you and your heart being a part of it. Thank you so much!

To my wife, Ellen, I say thanks for being such a critical part of everything I do. Life itself takes on new meaning every day you are by my side. I cherish and thank God for our life together. To Tyler, Seth, Catherine, Raelyn May and Tripp Tyler, you are the heartbeat of my life, the soul that gives me purpose and the joy that makes me smile each and every day!

Contents

Introduction

WHEN MY COUSIN PAULA WAS JUST A TODDLER, SHE COULD NOT PRONOUNCE my father's name, Everett. Instead, she called him "Habey." After hearing this as a young boy, I also affectionately called my dad Habey.

Dad was a rare breed. *Kind, patient, wise, unassuming, faith-centered, humble, funny, solid, savvy, generous, successful* (while at the same time ornery)—these are a few of the words that defined him. He was loved by his grandchildren, cherished by his children, adored by his wife, and respected by all who knew him. The dreaded disease of Alzheimer's robbed him of his last years; yet even in the hold of the disease, Habey's grace was evident.

As I have gotten older, I realize how blessed I was to be raised by two incredible people like Eileen and Everett Daniels. They navigated life together in an amazing way for over sixty-five years. Certainly, the way they modeled life provided the foundation of all that I have become; every accomplishment in my life was influenced greatly by those two wonderful people. After 37 years of ministry and witnessing the lack of effective parenting in many persons' lives, I have deep gratitude for my parents and their influence upon my life.

My dad was my confidant, mentor, hero, and one of my best friends. A few years ago, it occurred to me that many of the principles that guide my life came from conversations and experiences I had with my father. When I shared these principles with my wife, we began to call them "Habeyisms." She suggested I write them down for posterity because they ought to be passed on to our sons. So I kept a journal handy and began to write down the principles that Habey had given me. Little by little, I began to recall the circumstances surrounding the moments when these life principles had been shared. It amazed me how vivid those memories were.

Dad's principles were really ingenious. They were anything but simple and made his life anything but ordinary. When I later heard management and leadership gurus use similar principles in their workshops and books, I realized that others might benefit from my dad's insights as well. In their book, *A Leader's Legacy*, Kouzes and Posner wrote, "Our teachers continue to teach as we go on to tell their stories" (Kouzes and Posner 2006, 24). That's how this book was born. I hope that as you engage in these stories, my father's wisdom, character, and common sense will be shared over and over. In this way, his legacy will continue even though his physical existence has ended.

As the years go by, we learn that we do not leave a lasting legacy by chance, but by conscious intent. The traits of integrity, generosity, compassion, and grace can exert a powerful influence upon others if we call attention to them. Those words describe my dad. Everett Daniels was a good and decent man whose faith and character guided his actions. He always saw the good in others, and his consistent efforts to call forth the best in them made this world a better place.

While growing up on a farm, I learned that completing a task is much simpler if you have the right tool to accomplish it. Leaving a legacy is no different. The principles shared in this book are tools you can use to become a cherished legacy maker. My challenge to you is to take a firm hold of these principles to live your life purposefully to create a lasting legacy.

Legacy Maker is not difficult to read. It is simply the sharing of insightful experiences that took place between a father and son. These experiences shaped my life as I watched my father respond to life and its challenges with extraordinary grace. The principles behind them need not be difficult to live out; they need only to be practiced with clear intent.

These principles are transforming not only for individuals but for teams and organizations as well. It's amazing what can happen, even in big business, when a simple but profound principle is put into action.

Although I invite you to think in simple terms, watch for powerful results to take place.

Thank you in advance for allowing me to share this incredible man I had the privilege of calling my dad. I hope you capture some of his love and goodness as you read. I also trust you will share these principles with others along your life journey. All of us have the potential to pour wisdom into others; make this a priority of your life and take the time necessary to do it. Plant truth in others, as Habey did in me, and watch what happens.

You will find questions at the end of each chapter to help you reflect on what you have learned. These will also be helpful when you discuss these principles with teams in the workplace, small groups at church, or in family settings at home. Learning and growth occur exponentially as we learn together.

Gratefully and humbly yours,
Rolland Daniels
Pendleton, Indiana

It Never Costs Any More to Be Kind

The Power of the Golden Rule

WHEN I WAS ABOUT THE AGE OF TEN OR ELEVEN, MY DAD AND I WERE sitting in a restaurant where our waitress was stressed because she had too many customers and they were getting restless. In particular, one lady seemed determined to make a difficult situation worse. She was complaining at every opportunity. With every interaction, she spoke rudely to this young woman or criticized her in some way. If there were ever a reason for a waitress to "accidentally" spill a glass of water or bowl of chili into a customer's lap, this was it.

During it all, my dad just kept being cordial and even making jokes with the frazzled young woman. Yes, our food was late and somewhat cold, but that didn't seem to faze him. He seemed intent on making certain that this young lady knew someone was in her corner. This seemed to energize her. At the end of our meal, he went beyond generous and left her a very substantial tip.

We happened to leave the restaurant at the same time the more critical woman left. Even as she left, she attempted to trouble the waitress even further by asking to speak to the manager. However, my dad told the cashier what a fine job the young waitress was doing and cast a vote of confidence her way.

My dad walked out the door shaking his head. He stopped before getting in the car, placed his hand on the roof, and said, "Rolland, I want you to remember something. It never costs anyone any more to be kind."

That was my dad. I don't think I ever saw him criticize another person in public. He acted with grace and charity in all that he did, but I have always remembered that moment in the restaurant with uncommon clarity. Perhaps it is because I have a tendency to be critical and impatient, or because I was simply amazed by my dad's capacity to be good and kind. It is probably a little of both.

The Bible has a verse that well describes my father's kindness. It is called the Golden Rule and in it, Jesus states, "Treat people the same way you want them to treat you" (Matt. 7:12 NASV)." Why do you suppose we attribute so much importance to this principle that we call it "golden"? I think it's because this statement describes how we should relate to one another, and most of the difficult issues we face are rooted in faulty relationships with others.

A mentor in ministry once told me, "Rolland, the ministry wouldn't be so bad if it weren't for people." He said this as a joke, but it contained a vital truth. Look back over your life to see how many of your greatest struggles began because you responded negatively to other people or they responded negatively to you.

Jesus gave us the Golden Rule to reveal how our faith should influence our dealings with others. It is simple and straightforward: Treat people the way you want to be treated. There is not a lot of theological jargon here. Anyone can understand how living the Golden Rule makes a difference in our lives and the lives of people we know. It is easy to read, understand, and live out. Yes, we all have our moments of failure—even our days. However, our lives can be grounded in the choice to do good, be kind, and treat others fairly.

Every person has an endless supply of kindness. However, we must make the effort to mine and refine it. If we take that initiative, we will never run out of the compassion necessary to meet the endless challenges of life. Let's be honest, some of our mines of kindness seem to have played out; but that is not from lack of supply. It comes from our lack of effort to bring it forth. Our kindness varies in direct proportion to our willingness to demonstrate it.

> KINDNESS AND RUDENESS ARE TRAITS WHICH
> CAN BE LEARNED AND UNLEARNED.

Some of us might say that kindness was never modeled for us, therefore we are limited in our ability to be kind to others. The truth is, both kindness and rudeness are traits that can be learned and unlearned. Each of us has just as much ability to be kind as to be rude. It is not because we are physically gifted one way or the other. It is because we have chosen to live in a particular manner.

In high school, I played basketball and was a terrible free-throw shooter. However, my free-throw percentage would have been worse if I had shot left-handed and not with my dominant right hand. In the case of kindness, it is not a matter of physical dominance or even giftedness, but which trait we choose to bring forth and make dominant in our lives. Our supply of kindness is limited only by our efforts to express kindness in our relationships with others.

Thaddeus Barnum, in his book *Real Identity*, tells the moving story of a young man with Down syndrome. One Sunday morning, the children's ministry at the boy's church presented a modern-day version of the parable of the Good Samaritan. In one of the scenes, a child was riding her bike and had a nasty fall. Another child came walking by, witnessed the young girl hurt by the fall, and continued walking as she passed by without showing any concern.

The young man with Down syndrome was sitting in the audience and could not contain himself. He got up from his seat, quickly made his way down the aisle, and helped the young girl back on her bike. The children were upset because he interrupted their play, so they started the play all over again in the interest of getting the story right.

When the girl fell off the bike again, the gentle-hearted young man came running back down the aisle. But this time, as soon as he saw she was OK, he said in a rather loud but kind voice, "You've got to stop falling now." The church loved it and understood the heart from which it was delivered.

In truth, the young man's interruption of the parable could not have proven the story any more convincingly. His response of kindness to the young girl demonstrated he could not sit and do otherwise. In our shortsightedness, we might say, "This is a special situation with a unique and wonderful young man; such kindness cannot be displayed or lived out in the world such as we live and work" (Barnum 2013, 336). But that would mistake kindness for weakness or compassion for lack of tenacity. We need to be aware that kindness rests on the strength to show mercy when we could have shown anger or retribution. Many people fail to control the impulsive emotions of the moment and react to others with anger instead of kindness. But kindness enables us to say in strength, "You've got to stop falling now," or, as Jesus said to the woman caught in adultery, "Go and sin no more." Only by choosing to respond in kindness will we be able to avail ourselves of opportunities for strength. Remember, our kindness is limited only by our efforts to demonstrate kindness in our relationships with others.

Second, kindness is a boundless resource because there are endless opportunities to express kindness toward others. No matter what situation you find yourself in, you can be kind. Each day that you open your eyes to life, you will find situations where kindness is needed. Perhaps this equation defines it best:

Kindness Equation
Every Person + Endless Supply + Endless Opportunities = Golden Rule

You can't ask for a simpler statement of relational truth. Over and over, we witness situations where kindness is never expressed or received. All of us know office settings where the principle of kindness would revolutionize the environment. We have all been served at fast-food restaurants where kindness and courtesy would have changed our dining experience.

I walked down the aisle of a store yesterday and passed three employees, not one of whom spoke a word to me. In another aisle, two employees spoke critically of their manager, loudly enough for me and other customers to hear. Imagine, if you will, what simple kindness would do in such a situation. It could transform a dysfunctional culture into a more functional and inviting one. That is the kind of power kindness has.

Some of us exist in marriages and families where kindness is never expressed or experienced. (I could have said that some of us *live* in such situations, but in most marriages and families lacking kindness, the individuals exist rather than live.) Simple acts and words of kindness could change these dysfunctional or destructive relationships into life-giving ones. Instead, many people choose simply to tolerate one another and rudeness becomes the consistent trait of the home. Remember, rudeness is a learned trait and can be unlearned as well.

Les Parrott, in his book *3 Seconds*, cites research that highlights the power that caring and kindness have in the business world.

> Over 400 executives of the nation's largest companies in a variety of fields answered a survey by the Opinion Research Corporation on how they chose an airline for frequent travels. The executives rated a number of factors. And more than prompt baggage delivery or efficient check in, the aspect that mattered most to the vast majority was how much an airline "cares about its customers."
>
> We all know how much we as customers value caring service. I'm talking about personal service, the kind that is delivered by a real, live person, either behind the sales counter or at the end of the telephone. Caring is the difference between a confident nod with,

"Let's see what I can do for you," versus a shrug of the shoulders with, "There's nothing I can do for you."

In another survey, by William Wilsted, an adviser to Ernst and Young, the accounting and consulting firm, customers in banking, high-tech, and manufacturing considered "the personal touch" – the company's representative's commitment and whether he or she remembered a customer's name - to be the most important element of service. It beat out all the other factors, even convenience, speed of delivery, and how well the product worked (Parrott 2007, 41–42).

Stop for just a moment and ponder this question: *What simple act could I do today to bring good to another person's life at my workplace, on my team, or in my home?* Trust me, this act doesn't have to be complicated or costly. It simply has to be genuine and without selfish motives. If you repeat this simple initiative over time, the results will astonish you. I am a firm believer that *goodness and kindness beget goodness and kindness.* The truth is this: No matter the situation, it doesn't cost any more to be kind, yet the outcome can be transformational.

A few years ago, I was back in Collinsville, Mississippi, visiting the family homeplace where my dad and mom still lived at the time. I noticed a man I had known from my days as a teenager standing at his place of work. He had lived in what some might describe as a tainted manner. Many broken relationships had been left in his wake. I pulled over to speak with him since I hadn't seen him in thirty years, although at one time I considered him to be a friend.

As our conversation progressed, he asked about my dad. I told him Dad was doing fairly well, that the Alzheimer's disease was progressing slowly, but Dad still had a sense of humor. Then I noticed that his eyes were welling up with tears. He said, "Rolland, your dad has always been kind to me and treated me with respect. No matter where he saw me or who I was with, he always called me by name and talked with me. That has always meant a great deal to me."

KINDNESS HAS TO BE GENUINE
AND WITHOUT SELFISH MOTIVES.

Here we stood—a naïve boy now grown and a man whom some would consider calloused and cold, crying because the boy's father had shown him kindness. Remember, each of us has endless opportunities to do good to others.

A life of kindness is a matter of choice. These choices present themselves whenever we interact with people in daily life situations. It is in those moments that we can make a conscious choice to live with the dominant trait of kindness rather than rudeness.

As human beings, we determine most of the paths we take. Certainly, there are some paths we don't choose, such as poor health and tragic accidents; however, even then we can choose to treat others with kindness and grace. Yes, all of us can have an off day; but overall we have the power to choose that our lives will be full of kindness, with the Golden Rule consistently evident by the manner in which we live.

For those people who say, "I'm sorry, that is just not the way I am," I say, "Not true." You live in a rude and critical manner because you have chosen to do so. It is not the way you are; it is the way you choose to be. It is not because your personality is the inevitable product of your past experiences; it is because you act and feel this way in the present.

While I was growing up, one woman had a huge influence on my family's life. I'll call her Aunt Betty, although this was not her name and she had no biological relation to me. Aunt Betty was the type of person who was positive and always stood beside people in difficult times. If you were under the weather, Aunt Betty's homemade chicken dumplings would soon be at your door. Sometimes during Sunday worship, her hearing aid would make a shrill sound. (I grew up in a church where hearing aids were plentiful and they often went off, sounding like tea kettles brewing hot water!) Everyone could hear the hearing aid but Aunt Betty, so our pastor would kindly ask her to turn it down; Aunt Betty would chuckle to herself and we would get back to the order of worship. She was an exceptional woman.

But to really appreciate Betty's sweet spirit, one has to know where she came from. While Aunt Betty had two young children, her husband left her for another woman. In the process, Aunt Betty was abandoned with no place to go and no one to turn to for help. To say it was not easy would be a gross understatement. Yet she persevered and her faith carried her through very dark and difficult times.

Betty's story doesn't end there. Many years later, the husband who left her and the woman he left her for were both diagnosed with terminal cancer. This is when Aunt Betty's kindness shone. She brought the two of them to her home and cared for them both until they passed. Betty is a prime example that our past hurt and brokenness need not deter us from a life of kindness in the present. Remember the kindness equation:

Every Person + Endless Supply + Endless Opportunities = Golden Rule

There is not one person to whom this equation does not apply. Some may say, "This is not how I was taught," or, "Life has dealt me a rotten hand." That may be the case, yet the good news is this: You can change the way you respond to life. You can look deep inside yourself and draw out kindness. Every time one of these difficult situations confronts you, you can act on this truth: It doesn't cost any more to be kind. My dad was right. It takes only a little effort, but it will make a world of difference in your life and in the lives of others.

Kindness needs only to be practiced in order to give life to others. Begin intentionally bringing forth kindness in your life today and see what fruit it might bear. Determine that your place of business will see more examples of kindness than of rudeness. Live ever aware that life is filled with golden opportunities to make kindness a dominant trait in your relationships with others.

Discussion Questions

1. Was the trait of kindness modeled for you while growing up? How?
2. Are there places in your life where the trait of kindness is still missing or random?
3. What steps could you and others take to make kindness an ongoing part of your environment? For example, if you are part of a team at your workplace, how can you demonstrate kindness toward your co-workers?
4. How would this change your environment for the good?
5. How much will taking those steps cost you?

2 CHAPTER

Having Everything Doesn't Guarantee Anything

The Power of Understanding What Matters Most

Do you remember the day Elvis Presley died? I do. I was standing in my mom and dad's living room when the breaking news came across their old Motorola television set. Certainly, Elvis was one of the greatest entertainers the world has ever known. He was wealthy beyond measure and loved (some say worshipped) by millions of people. On the day he died, there was a great sense of sadness and loss across the world. Not only was Elvis an entertainment icon and relatively young when he died, but he was a lonely man.

As my dad and I watched news updates about the singer's death, I struggled to understand how a man with so much felt as though he had so little. After some time, my dad said, "Rolland, there are people in this world who seem to have everything and yet, when you look closer, they have nothing. On the other hand, some people have nothing in the material sense and yet have everything when it comes to happiness and fulfillment. The truth is, having everything doesn't guarantee anything."

All of us have witnessed the tragic results of a life lived with little or no understanding of what it truly means to live. Equally tragic are people who live with little or no appreciation for what they have. At times, we have all been guilty of this. We wish we could say we had given our lives the best efforts and priorities all the way through, but in truth we can't. Most of us have passed through seasons when we did not put forth our best. Some of us did not even consider our best as the benchmark for life. Such people simply muddle through life with no serious thought of achieving anything beyond mediocrity, and their current situations reflect that.

However, one of the wonderful things about the journey of life is that redemption and transformation are always possible. Lamentations 3:22–23 states, "Through the LORD's mercies we are not consumed, Because His compassions fail not. They are new every morning; Great is Your faithfulness" (NKJV). The writer makes clear that the Lord's mercy and loving-kindness can keep our second-class efforts from consuming us.

If we reflect honestly on our lives, we remember when our least and worst efforts were noticeable. We may even realize that our lives sometimes teetered on the brink of consumption. Even then, we could reclaim our lives as we renewed our intentions to live with greater purpose and meaning. Something inside us resonates deeply with the notion that our least and worst will no longer suffice. We can no longer be satisfied with just "getting by," so we determine that we will no longer give just that to our marriages, our jobs, our parenting efforts, or manner of living. Because the gift of life deserves better. we determine to live with a new reality at the helm. For most of us, divine inspiration is involved in such a realization.

Our lives seldom change without some significant life event taking place. We have made it as far as we can on our own and we have run our ship aground again and again. Perhaps a life tragedy has stopped us in our tracks and we recognize our need for something or Someone else to help us navigate our course. Whatever the case, the proverbial two-by-four has gotten our attention and we begin to reevaluate what it truly means to live. In sometimes painful ways, we are given the chance to reassess and reevaluate what we are doing with the gift God has given us. From this point on, we have the opportunity to pursue different and better courses. In looking back, we recognize that the path to redemption has not been taken without some costs attached.

Others of us are fortunate to have people enter our lives with insights that helped to light our journey. Perhaps we asked them to serve as our guides along the way and they steered us to a fruitful life. Perhaps we were painfully aware that we had not lived a perfect life, even with capable mentors and guides, but our advantages far outweighed the disadvantages. If this is your story, then consider yourself blessed.

As I have gotten older, I recognize the blessing of having significant people shape my life. My dad was certainly one of them. He was a successful businessman and my family benefitted from that. However, Dad never made money the ultimate goal of his life or his accomplishments the topic of his conversations. My father was just a good and generous man, and he put before me some specific life priorities.

First, his faith influenced his actions. Dad was not one who tried to convince others to adopt his beliefs, but his consistent lifestyle made what he believed very evident. Over the years, I watched him care for and give to others, with no recognition of what he was doing. This instilled in me the truth that our resources should be used to bless others and our faith is better practiced than simply talked about.

WHAT YOU SAY MATTERS VERY LITTLE
IF IT DOES NOT CORRELATE WITH WHAT YOU DO.

We have all known people who speak boldly of faith, but their words and actions are so saturated with anger and bitterness that they are repellant to others. We also have known those who profess faith, yet their lifestyle doesn't affirm their words at all. These people demonstrate that what you say matters very little if it does not correlate with what you do. My father's faith and life had a harmonious rhythm that he shared throughout his life.

Second, the importance of family was a constant in my dad's life. The family unit is defined in many different ways today, yet I believe that our families deserve our presence and attention. An individual who truly values something or someone will invest himself in that relationship. Presence and attention represent a sacrificial giving of ourselves. Presence and attention are priorities that every one of us can exemplify. Our presence and attention will determine the worth felt by those within our families.

On the other hand, a lack of our presence and attention will result in the exact opposite. Our family members who do not receive them will feel devalued and disrespected. Continued presence and attention build a deep sense of wholeness within a family, while their absence creates dysfunction and bitterness.

As I reflect on my childhood, I don't remember any school function that involved my sister, brother, or me that both of our parents did not attend. Their presence and attention demonstrated our value and worth in an obvious way. When parents consistently give their presence to their children, they show that they have ultimate value. That is true for all families.

WHEN PARENTS GIVE THEIR PRESENCE TO THEIR CHILDREN,
THEY SHOW THAT THEY HAVE ULTIMATE VALUE.

The Bible addresses that issue in Isaiah 55:2, "Why waste your money on what really isn't food? Why work hard for something that doesn't satisfy?" (NLT). I deeply respected my dad's ability to rightly define what really had value and what didn't. He made choices to intentionally pursue the things that cultivated meaning and fulfillment in others' lives.

Did my dad work hard to make a living? Yes. Did my dad make good money? Yes. Was he consumed with it and did it define him? No.

He was much more concerned with spending quality time with those he loved and using his resources to benefit others. In some ways, I am still awed at his capacity to accept who he was and who he was not. There is a deep-seated peace within those individuals like my dad who have rightly discerned that happiness, contentment, and meaning are things money cannot buy.

We all know people whose lives are in emotional and relational shambles because they have fed their egos or tried to fulfill their needs with things that don't truly satisfy. Some look the part of success and wholeness; but a closer examination reveals deep insecurities and an inner angst that power, position, and material things cannot cover up.

I have never seen this more clearly exemplified than on the unfortunate occasion when, as a minister, I had two memorial services in one day. One funeral was for one of the richest men in our city, who was said to own so much land across the United States that he could not remember all the particular parcels of land at his disposal. Yet his memorial service was one of the saddest occasions I can remember.

His family sat on both sides of the chapel and none of the parties involved were on speaking terms with one another. With his passing, the business of wills and inheritance dominated their relationships. It was evident that his family had learned well the greed and gain he had exemplified. The mood in the chapel that day was not one of grief, but of calculation and manipulation. I saw no effort to console one another or embrace each other's pain. The memorial service was simply a ritual that allowed them to look the part of a caring family before meeting with the attorney to see what had been left to each of them. I will never forget the emotional and relational frigidity of that day.

Few of this man's friends were in attendance. He was well known to use people and then discard them without another thought. The service was a stark reminder of a man whose life was but a shell of what it could have been. He had given his life to acquiring things that couldn't truly satisfy and that legacy had been passed down to those his life had touched. That funeral reminded me vividly of my father's insight, "Having everything doesn't guarantee anything."

As I drove to the second service, I wondered what awaited me. The second memorial service was for a local farmer who owned very little. To supplement his farming income, he also drove a school bus for over thirty years.

I walked into the sanctuary and watched his family sitting together. The dynamics were completely different than those of the first memorial service. The farmer's family and friends shared their grief by embracing and consoling one another. There were laughter and tears as they shared common stories from their past. Multiple generations were present and shared in the story telling. It was evident that the man had devoted his presence and attention to those he loved, which truly brought value and meaning to their lives.

Also, I was astonished to see how many non-family members who attended. Many former students who had ridden this farmer's bus came to pay their respects. They wanted his family to know how kind and special he had been as their bus driver. One by one, people greeted the family and shared stories of how he had helped them in times of need without anyone else knowing. His life had been built upon caring and generosity.

I marveled that day at the stark differences between the two funeral services. The first reflected a man who had everything and yet, in a deeper sense, had nothing. The second reflected a gentleman who had very few material things, yet had everything of genuine value because of how he invested his life.

Please understand, I am not saying that money is a bad thing or that those who have wealth are bad people. As my dad once told me, "Money isn't everything, but it sure helps you be miserable." Some of the most generous and gracious people I have ever known were wealthy, but they knew there are some things money can't buy. So they invested in what truly satisfies and endures.

God does care about what we do with what we have. It is like any parent with a child. Do we lavish gifts on our children so that they can become selfish and spoiled brats? Of course not. We give them gifts because we love them; but we watch carefully how they handle those gifts. How they use those resources tells us much about the kind of people they are growing up to be.

The truth is, our children's character and integrity will never be determined by what they have. It will be determined by what they do with what they have. Are they selfish toward other people, or are they generous in sharing what has been given them? We learn so much about their character and their hearts in this way. Those traits are what we are ultimately concerned about, and those traits are ultimately what God is concerned about.

I recently read a review of the book, *Measure What Matters: How Google, Bono, and the Gates Foundation Rock the World with OKRs* (Doer, 2018). The review was written by Todd Wilson (2018) of Exponential Ministries, who described his recent journey through critical medical problems that could have taken his life. That experience had caused him to ponder some serious questions:

> I find myself asking, "Am I being the best possible steward of the time, talents, and treasures that God has blessed me with? Am I focused primarily on pursuing a legacy by *what* I build, accumulate and leave behind, or by *who* I invest in and catapult forward to the next generation?" You might summarize all these questions with this question, "Am I measuring here on earth what matters most in the scorecard of eternity?" (Wilson, 2018).

In response to this season of self-assessment, Wilson has given himself to living out some axioms that his mentor, Bob Buford, passed down to him:

- "I want to focus on giving others permission, encouragement, applause, and accountability for 100X impact!"
- "I'm the catapult, not the plane."
- "My fruit grows on other people's trees."
- "You can do it; how can I help?" (Wilson, 2018)

Rob Reiner's film, *The Bucket List*, starring Morgan Freeman and Jack Nicholson, is a great example of this principle. As both men's characters are diagnosed with terminal cancer, they set out on a journey to fulfill the bucket list of their lives. Each man enters the journey at a completely different place.

Morgan's character has lived his life as a committed husband, father, and grandfather. He is a man who has given himself completely to his family and is now receiving a return on that investment. The monument of his legacy is not what he owns, but how he has touched and invested in the lives of others. Nicholson's character is a man of extreme wealth who has lived his life only for himself and now his most precious possession is a rare coffee urn. You get the gist of the differences represented.

At one moment in their journey, Freeman's character explains to Nicholson's the two questions that the ancient Egyptians were asked before being permitted to enter heaven: Have you found joy in your life? And have you brought joy to someone else's life?

Nicholson's character cannot answer the second question. His life has been lived only for himself and what he could gain. Other people were a necessary bother to him. Yet, at the end of the movie, the audience witnesses this unique friendship created by tragedy do something extraordinary in Nicholson's character's life. In his words, the friendship saved his life even in the face of death by showing him that there was more to life than things. He felt their friendship exemplified the joy of giving to others. It is amazing that sometimes great tragedy causes us to see the beauty of that which has always been around us.

Most of us have heard of Stephen King, a prolific writer whose books have turned into blockbuster movies. However, what you and I may not know is that in 1999 when he was walking along the side of a road, he was struck by a van. During the time that he was at death's door, he learned some of life's most valuable lessons. In the November 1, 2001 *Family Circle* magazine, King penned an article titled, "What You Pass On," that included these thoughts:

I had my MasterCard in my wallet, but when you're lying in a ditch with broken glass in your hair, no one accepts MasterCard. On that day and in the following months I got some painful but very important insights into many of life's simple truths. The first one was this. We came into this life naked and broke and we may be dressed when we go out but we're still just as broke. Of all the power that we have in this country, so blessed that we are, the greatest power that we have is undoubtedly the power to show compassion and the ability to give. We have enormous resources, but they are only yours and mine on loan. They are only yours to give for a short while.

What I want you to consider is to make your life one long gift of giving to others. Why not? Because all we have is on loan anyway (King 2001, 156).

Each of us has a choice about what we invest our lives in. It has nothing to do with our take-home pay or position of achievement. It has everything to do with understanding and heeding the truth that "having everything doesn't guarantee anything." My hope is that we will not wait for tragedy to bring us to our senses. It is important that we reassess what has given value to our lives and to whom have we given value. We can begin by asking, how have we invested our presence and attention?

Discussion Questions

1. What has defined joy, meaning, and fulfillment in your life? Things? Position? Money? Relationships? Serving/Sharing? Generosity?
2. In what way have you valued and brought joy to someone else's life?
3. How has your presence and attention been evident to them?
4. At this point, which of the two memorial services would define your life?
5. What do you need to do to change the trajectory of your life?

People Move People

The Power of Connections

MY FATHER AND UNCLE OWNED A ROOFING CONSTRUCTION BUSINESS, AND both were astute businessmen. They grew the roofing corporation my grandfather started into one of the largest family-owned operations in the Southeast. It was a business built on hard work and relationships of trust and integrity. Every Christmas, they would load the trunks of their cars with hams and deliver them personally to every contractor they did business with to show appreciation.

As a young boy, I often made this annual journey with my dad, who drove all over the state of Mississippi and parts of Alabama dropping off hams. We would leave very early in the morning and not return until very late at night. On one particular day, the trip seemed especially long and boring to me. With each stop, my dad spent more time talking with more people than I thought necessary. He talked with everyone in each office and seemed to know them each by name. Finally, in my weariness, I asked Dad why he didn't just mail or ship the hams with a personal letter of thanks attached to each one.

Dad didn't hesitate with his answer and his response still influences the way I lead today. He said, "Rolland, paper doesn't move people; people move people."

He continued, "Rolland, I never send a letter when I can send myself. Nothing matters as much as making the effort to look a person in the eye and say, 'Thank you for giving us your business.'"

My dad entered the Navy upon his completion of high school to serve during World War II. He was not able to attend his high school graduation because he had to report to boot camp instead. After finishing his tour of duty, he continued working in the family roofing business. His "college" education consisted of long hours, hot days, and on-the-job training. He became an exceptional businessman. We would refer to him today as someone who possessed a high EQ (emotional quotient). His ability to relate to and understand people was key to his success. In a day before books and conferences teaching how to close a deal or influence people, my dad's innate understanding allowed him to successfully do all those things. Perhaps a fundamental factor to his success was that he understood and lived out the powerful principle that people move people.

In a time when our culture is defined by personal disconnectedness and the alienation of isolation, people long for a personal touch or a personal word spoken to them. More and more, cell phone family plans, texting, and Snapchat are replacing face-to-face conversations. At lunch the other day, I sat across from a family of four in which each person was texting on their cell phone but not personally interacting with each other. This was a vivid example of the alienation of isolation, even in the company of others. It is no wonder that Facetime and video conferencing are growing more and more popular each day. It is also why employers are desperate to find job candidates with good "people skills." People desire to talk to a human face instead of seeing words scroll on a screen or hearing faceless words spoken. Despite our marvelous digital communications technology, human interaction is still so very important. The simple reason: People move people.

Don't get me wrong, I am not the sort of fellow who despises technology or wishes things would always stay the same. In fact, I Facebook, Facetime, Skype, Instagram, blog, Zoom, Twitter, Snapchat, and text! Yet, as I grow older and more seasoned by life, I realize that my father was brilliant in a common-sense kind of way because he understood the importance of personal connections.

The writer of Proverbs states the principle this way, "Know your sheep by name; carefully attend to your flocks (Prov. 27:23, The Message)." Many of us remember the commercial that depicted a CEO whose company was struggling. He responded by gathering his employees and passing out airline tickets so they could meet their clients face-to-face. He was taking his company back to the basic understanding that people move people. In essence, he was instructing his company to know their clients by name and better attend to them.

It is easy to understand why many businesses and families flounder today. They do not share enough personal words of affirmation or personal touches in their relationships. Somewhere along the line, they have lost their way and forgotten what really matters. The principle of connecting emotionally, physically, or relationally is not easy for some people. They were never told nor shown the basic needs of human existence—love, care, value, respect, affirmation, and appreciation. They were raised in the world of Distant and dropped off at the corner of Critical and Withdrawn.

Others have allowed busyness to absorb the time for personal engagement. They have fooled themselves into believing affection and affirmation don't matter that much. The tragedy is that the fooled has become the fool. Families fall apart for lack of affection and affirmation. Marriages die on the vine for lack of sincere affirmation from one spouse to another. Clients leave because another company is more attentive to their needs. A parent looks around and realizes a son or daughter is isolated because a meaningful relationship has not been intentionally cultivated. In one way or another, these scenarios represent people who have forgotten the basic principle that people move people.

But it doesn't have to be this way. We can determine to invest ourselves in one another. We can realize that something very basic and necessary is missing from our lives. Each of us can remind ourselves that, just as our physical bodies must have food and water for survival, our emotional and relational needs can be met by love, care, value, respect, appreciation, and affirmation. The human being responsible for meeting these needs is the person we see in the mirror every day.

Some responsibilities cannot be abdicated or delegated to others. A parent texting a message of love to a child cannot replace a physical hug or personal words spoken to that child. Emailing words of devotion to our spouse cannot replace holding the hand of our beloved while taking a slow walk on the beach. A boss can email deep appreciation for a job well done, but nothing takes the place of walking down the hall and sharing that appreciation personally, especially in the presence of others.

I love those moments on television when a man or woman who has been serving our country overseas returns unexpectedly to his or her loved ones. The moment a veteran's spouse or child recognizes who it is, they make a spontaneous, exuberant effort to reach them. Rest assured, most of these service women and men have skyped, emailed, called, or written their families during their time overseas. But nothing, absolutely nothing, replaces the affection and affirmation of a physical touch or a word spoken in person.

I once heard of a boss who sent a note to an employee, expressing thanks for a job well done. On the back of the note, the boss asked that person to pass it along to the other offices in order to save time. He had no idea that for efficiency's sake he had missed the opportunity to move people. Instead, his gesture expressed to each employee that his time was more valuable than they were. Trust me, his genuine appreciation was lost in the lack of personal interaction. He sorely forgot that people move people.

Some of us respond easily to this challenge to express affection and affirmation, while others are more reserved. For the benefit of all, here are some simple suggestions for making this principle more applicable in your life.

Assess your Relationships

Take an assessment of your relationships and identify the people you need to appreciate and affirm the most. Are you prioritizing your time in a way that allows you to deliver this important message on a regular basis? I urge you to make your family the priority. Every husband and wife, father and mother should realize that their relationship to each other and to their children cannot be delegated to others or postponed to another time. It is critical that family members regularly engage each other in order to keep balanced, emotionally healthy, and focused on the right priorities.

Our two sons are different in many ways. Tyler, our oldest, is more reserved and processes information over time, not in moments. He builds deep relationships and loyalty is always a strong characteristic in each of those ties. Seth, our youngest, is more gregarious and processes change more quickly. He is an organizer who even organized my desk when he was a young child!

My wife Ellen and I had to learn how to relate to our sons in different ways to accommodate their differences. This took a good deal of trial and error, which I believe is true for all parents and spouses. If we desire to move those key relationships toward a positive outcome, then we will need to invest the necessary time and thought. Rick Warren writes regarding time,

> Time is your most precious gift because you only have a set amount of it. You can make more money, but you can't make more time. When you give someone your time, you are giving them a portion of your life that you'll never get back. Your time is your life. That is why the greatest gift you can give someone is your time. It is not enough to just say relationships are important; we must prove it by investing time in them. Words alone are worthless. "My children, our love should not be words and talk; it must be true love, which shows itself in action." Relationships, time and effort, and the best way to spell love is "T-I-M-E" (Warren 2002, 127).

When our youngest son, Seth, was just a small boy, he understood the importance of giving someone your undivided attention. If we were in a conversation together and he felt I wasn't paying close enough attention, he would crawl up in my lap and take my face in his hands. He would turn my face until it was directly lined up with his and then ask, "Can you hear me now, Daddy?"

I would answer, "Yes."

"Good," he would respond, "because you weren't hearing me before."

I wasn't having trouble hearing him; I was having trouble giving him my undivided attention and affection. Many of us frequently struggle with this. For this reason, take the initiative and have breakfast on a Saturday with your son or daughter just to listen, not to share your desires for them or critique what they are doing or not doing. Let your spouse sleep in and make this a regular part of your monthly or bi-weekly routine. I took our sons out to breakfast regularly for 18 straight years until they both went off to college. And I am convinced it is one of the reasons we share the positive relationships we do today.

Another way to show your attention and affection is to practice spontaneous gifting. On your way home tomorrow, stop to get a card or small gift for your spouse just to show your appreciation. Even simple gestures like this make a powerful statement. Bring home their favorite donuts, the newest edition of their favorite sports magazine, or a bouquet of flowers. This can say powerfully that they were on your mind.

Every person wants to know personal appreciation. Set a weekly date night, no matter how long you have been married, and don't break the date. When Ellen and I were first married, we had little money. Many Friday nights, we would buy a large drink at McDonalds to share and spend two hours talking as we drove in the country. Some nights, Ellen would write down questions for us to ask each other as we drove. I never regretted spending those evenings together. We are now reaping the benefits of always choosing to spend time with each other. All of this comes down to the simple notion of priorities and choices. If we are not willing to make relationships a priority on our calendars, then these people will never feel they are a priority in our lives.

Define Who You Need to Move

Appreciation and affirmation are needed on our jobs as much as in our homes, but we need to be careful about how we offer them. Appreciation and affirmation should always be offered sincerely. Never say something simply to make someone feel good. In most cases, that is a form of manipulation. Affirm your co-workers or employees by rewarding what they do that is positive and productive. Remember, what gets affirmed is most likely to be repeated. Therefore, you are building a work culture that affirms what you would like to see repeated there. The commitment to affirm people daily does not take extra time or resources. It simply requires you to reallocate the time and resources you already use.

WHAT GETS AFFIRMED GETS REPEATED.

The truth is, none of us can impact every relationship we have in the same way, but all of us can impact the critical ones in crucial areas of our lives. At work, ask yourself this question: Who are five to ten people that I need to affect on a regular basis? After identifying those people, make an intentional effort every month to demonstrate one of the following traits to this group of people: care, value, respect, appreciation, and affirmation. If you are a manager or supervisor, walk the hallway and stick your head inside each office long enough to offer encouragement. Say it loud enough that others can hear you, because what gets affirmed gets repeated.

As you work to make this happen, you need to discern how to communicate love, care, respect, value, appreciation, and affirmation to each individual in your group on an ongoing basis. This means listening and learning the stories of your co-workers. Personal stories are important because our stories define who we are. In fact, they express our personalities. They influence how we interact with others, the words we use and how we share them. They affect our perceptions of others and even our perceptions of ourselves. Our stories even help to define what we value most and what moves us the most. Therefore, if we don't know an individual's story, we don't know how best to appreciate, affirm, and motivate that person to reach their best.

As I teach classes in leadership and organizational behavior, I often make this statement to the students, "If you don't take time to learn the stories of the people you lead, you will never lead them as effectively as you could." The reason: You will never know what makes them who they are, how best to motivate them, and how best to support them. Listening and learning stories are a critical role for every leader, no matter your context. It shows the people you lead that you value and care about them enough to listen.

I once spoke with a man who interacted with a hundred associates every month. Each month he would highlight the work of one individual in the group for going the extra mile or demonstrating loyalty to the team and organization. He was particular in how he phrased what he said about the individual so that he spoke uniquely to and about that person. The man was amazed at how the group would listen expectantly for the affirmation of that person and the celebration of the whole organization that would take place in response to that short moment of affirmation and recognition. This leader had discerned that all people desire affirmation and affection. He also knew the stories of those on his team because of his close engagement with them. He understood how to utilize the power of story to best affirm and appreciate those around him.

Another key is to celebrate victories with those on your team. Very few teams and organizations understand the importance of celebrating together. It builds morale and momentum, and it multiplies a positive atmosphere. All organizations have their struggles, but few take the opportunity to counterbalance struggles with celebration. Many times, we are so consumed with the next thing we forget to celebrate the effort and teamwork that it took to accomplish the current thing.

My wife and I had dinner with some friends the other night, one of whom was a very successful college basketball coach. This coach held team workouts at six o'clock in the morning during the week. Imagine the excitement her players had for those early morning workouts! However, the coach understood how difficult these workouts were and chose to bring a positive note to what could have been perceived as a negative. She told the team that by the following week, she and the assistant coach would learn a dance routine to a very popular song and perform it during one of that week's practices.

Trust me, no one was late for any practice that week. The anticipation was palpable. What was a struggle before became a moment of morale building and momentum for this team as the head coach and assistant pulled off the dance routine. Where there had been groans and moans there now were cheers and applause. Remember, we can contradict struggles with celebration, but we must take time to celebrate as a team.

The principle of people moving people can change the culture of many organizations, families, and teams. Intentional small gestures will make a great difference if lived out on a regular basis. This is true because at the crux of all human relations lies the truth that affection, appreciation, and affirmation are how people move people.

I remember one day sitting in my study with a couple who had been married for over thirty years. Just a couple of weeks before, the wife had told the husband that she wanted a divorce. The husband was distraught and asked his wife to set up an appointment to meet with me. For a while, I listened carefully to their very strained conversation. It was evident that the emotional relationship between the two was somewhere between nil and nothing. During the entire conversation, they looked at me but never at each other. Their words were dry and dead, spoken with no feeling or emotion.

Finally, I asked the wife, "If you could change one thing in your marriage, what would you change?"

Without hesitation, she said, "That he would tell me he loved me."

At this, the very docile husband exploded, "Love you?? I have worked hard for you for over thirty years to tell you I love you! What in the world do you expect from me?"

The woman now sat there, sobbing, "I just want you to look me in the eye and tell me you love me."

There it was, the culprit of this dying relationship. One spouse deeply needed love, care, value, respect, appreciation, and affirmation, while the other thought that hard work could replace appreciation shown through affectionate words and a loving touch. Knowing our family and friends by name and carefully attending them means working hard to understand their deepest emotional needs. It also means getting to know their personal stories. This does not happen by chance. It means discovering what heart language another person speaks and then being very intentional to speak that language on a regular basis. It means expressing appreciation, affirmation, and affection in intentional, tangible ways that display our understanding of the principle that people move people.

My father and uncle's customers certainly understood this because this life principle was ingrained in them and their company. The hours of driving simply to share five minutes of face time in order to more adequately express appreciation was a win-win for both employer and employee. These two men were not successful by chance. They understood hard work and the basic emotional needs that all human beings have, and they responded by meeting those needs. Remember the basic principle my dad understood and lived by: People move people. They always have. They always will.

Discussion Questions

1. Where has the principle that "people move people" been left out of your life?
2. What could you do to show affirmation and appreciation to those around you?
3. What excuses are you using to "cop out" of this responsibility?
4. Who will you ask to hold you accountable to move past these excuses?
5. How will you encourage others in your community/tribe to begin creating a "people move people" culture?

4 CHAPTER

Finish What You Start

The Power of Perseverance

IT WAS AUGUST IN MISSISSIPPI AND I WAS ABOUT TO START MY JUNIOR YEAR of high school. I had just finished working construction and baling hay throughout the summer. I was exhausted. The next morning, I had to report to start two-a-days for Fall football practice and the weariness took its toll.

Fatigue and weariness have the capacity to bend our will and sometimes even break our will. On this occasion, that was certainly true for me. I was so tired at the end of that first week I told the coach I was quitting. I didn't mention this decision to my parents over the weekend as I knew they would be disappointed. The following Monday morning at 6:30, my dad knocked on my bedroom door because practice began at 7:00. He said, "You need to get up, man. You are going to be late for practice."

I replied, "I am not going to practice. I quit football."

Dad walked away, only to return five minutes later, fully dressed. He told me to get out of bed. When I asked why, he said, "We are going to help reverse one of the worst decisions of your life."

"And what would that be?" I asked.

"Quitting," Dad said. "Now get out of bed and let's go."

Dressed and in the car a few minutes later, I got the rest of my dad's message. "Rolland, at the end of the season, if you decide you don't want to play football anymore, that will be fine. But there is one thing your mom and I expect of you as a part of this family: You will finish what you start. So we are going over to the school and you will apologize to the coach and your teammates. You will then ask if you can get back on the team and do whatever extra work you have to do to earn that right." With that, he personally drove me to the school and stood beside me while I spoke with the coach.

Then my crash course of eating humble pie began. I once heard the statement, "If you have to eat crow, then chew hard and swallow fast." That was my rule that Friday morning. Trust me, there was a lot of chewing and even more intense swallowing in store. If I thought that it was hot the day before, I didn't even know hot! On that day and every day for two weeks, I had to run 15 extra 100-yard belly-slam sprints. But I did my penance and got back on the team.

When I look back, I am thankful my dad made me return to football. It was not an easy choice, but the best choice I—or rather, my dad—ever made. We had a good year as a team, and I had more fun playing football that year than any other year I played. All because of my dad's expectation of me to finish what I started.

Over the years, I have tried to teach my sons the same lesson. I want them to understand how easy it is to quit and how easily quitting can become a habit. We have all known individuals who are habitual quitters. They quit on spouses, children, employers, and even God. If something doesn't go the right way or their toes get stepped on, they are on the first bus to "Outta There."

Deuteronomy 31:6 says, "Do not be afraid and do not panic... For the LORD your God will personally go ahead of you. He will neither fail you nor abandon you (NLT)." I have found this verse speaks very directly to my first reaction in difficult situations, to quit or run. This verse speaks directly about the cause, that element of fear. Many people suffer from fear, whether they admit it or not. They habitually respond with anxiety or apprehension when confronted with life's challenges. Fear drives them to take flight or quit too quickly.

This fear can play itself out in many ways in different people. For some, there is the tendency to fear that they won't measure up to the challenge. They believe that if others saw the real person inside, they would be despised. Others are perfectionists who believe that quitting or not trying is better than allowing others to discover that they are not perfect. Some live with the fear that the criticism of others might turn out to be true, or that their own low opinion of themselves might become reality. Fear can manifest itself in many other ways. The nature of fear can be as varied and unique as the individuals involved. However, the result is usually the same—escape.

When fear strikes, we panic. If you recognize what I am describing, then you have known those moments of panic. Then we want to flee. In fact, the process can become so habitual that it can become an unconscious, instinctive response. That is why quitting is so destructive and causes havoc in so many lives. Our fear causes us to panic, which then causes us to take flight. Instead of responding thoughtfully and calmly to the situation, we look for the exits. This never allows us to face, work through, and overcome our fears.

The second part of this verse has helped me overcome the fears that perfectionism and pride had created. I came to understand, through my failures much more than my successes, that I depended much more on the affirmation of others than on the power and faithfulness of God, who promised to go before me and with me.

In brokenness, I learned to find my fulfillment in the applause of One and not in the applause of many. I began to take hold of the truth that the last part of the Deuteronomy passage gives to us: *God will neither fail me nor abandon me.* There is Someone bigger than me and my problems. By trusting completely in God's steadfastness and faithfulness, my fears began to be replaced by trust in the unending faithfulness of God's love.

As I began to trust God's faithfulness, I was more willing to make myself vulnerable to intimate relationships with others. I gained the courage to risk failure without being paralyzed by the potential of disappointing others or disappointing my perfectionist self. I often say that I am a recovering perfectionist. Now my fulfillment is found in the One who promised never to fail me or abandon me. It is incredibly comforting to know the One who will not fail me or walk away from me.

A prime example of such trust is Peter's experience in Matthew 14, when he stepped out of the boat and walked on the water toward Jesus. At one point, his fear overcame his capacity to stay focused on the Source and he began to sink. This only illustrates that Peter is more like us than we know. But at Peter's moment of failure, Jesus pulled him out of the water. There is great security in knowing that even in our failures, God is ready to reach out to us.

This passage is also a great reminder that unless we step out of the comfort of our boat, we will never accomplish anything greater than we have known. To truly see the power of the divine in our very human lives; we must step out of our comfort zones and into the space where fear and pain must be conquered by faith in Someone greater than us.

Allow me to tell you about Kim Phuc. You have seen her picture a thousand times, but I doubt that you recognize her by name. Her picture was taken outside her Vietnamese village in 1972 by Associated Press photographer Nic Ut, for which he was given a Pulitzer Prize. It is also a photo that made the world take notice of that horrific war. The photo captured nine-year-old Kim Phuc running along a puddled roadway in front of an expressionless soldier. Her arms were outstretched, she was naked, and she shrieked in pain and fear as a napalm bomb exploded in the background.

Phuc was left with the crippling weight of anger, bitterness, and resentment toward those who caused her suffering. She suffered excruciating pain as multiple procedures were performed to help her heal physically. She expressed it well in an article in *Christianity Today* (May 2018):

> I craved relief that never would come. And yet, despite every last external circumstance that threatened to overtake me—mind, body, and soul—the most agonizing pain I suffered during that season of life

> dwelled in my heart. I was as alone as a person can
> be. I could not turn to a friend, for nobody wished to
> befriend me. I was toxic, and everyone knew it. To be
> near me was to be near hardship. Wise people stayed
> far away. I was alone, atop a mountain of rage. *Why was
> I made to wear these awful scars?* I grew up hearing the
> proverb "A tree wants to be alone, but the wind always
> whips it here and there." That was me: a wind-whipped
> tree. And I feared I would never stand upright again
> (Phuc 2018, 88).

In 1982, Kim Phuc found herself inside Saigon's central library, searching Vietnamese books of religion for some sense of purpose and meaning. The stack contained books of many religions and it also contained a copy of the New Testament. She thumbed through several books before opening the New Testament. A short time later, as she made her way through the Gospels, two themes touched her deeply.

First, she noted that Jesus' entire ministry pointed to one straightforward claim: "I am the way you get to God; there is no other way but me." Second, this Jesus knew suffering and pain. He too had been wounded and he too bore scars. The more she read, the more she came to believe that "He really was who He said He was, that He really had done what He said He had done, and that—most important to her—He really would do all that He had promised."

Fittingly enough, on Christmas Eve 1982, Phuc made her way to a Christmas Eve service at a small church in Saigon. The pastor spoke about how Christmas is not about the gifts we give to each other, but the gift we receive in Jesus. As she listened to this message, she knew that something was shifting inside her. She describes how deep this shift was.

> How desperately I needed peace. How ready I was for
> love and joy. I had so much hatred in my heart—so
> much bitterness. I wanted to let go of all my pain. I
> wanted to pursue life instead of holding fast to fantasies

of death. I wanted this Jesus. So, when the pastor finished speaking, I stood up, stepped out into the aisle, and made my way to the front of the sanctuary to say, yes, to Jesus Christ. And there, in a small church in Vietnam, mere miles from the street where my journey had begun amid the chaos of war—on the night before the world would celebrate the birth of the Messiah—I invited Jesus into my heart. When I woke up that Christmas morning, I experienced the kind of healing that can only come from God. I was finally at peace (Phuc 2018, 88).

Like most of us, Phuc needed something outside herself to enable her to overcome the hurt and pain of the past in order to move toward a bigger and greater future. Faith gave her the courage and strength not to quit or give in "to fantasies of death." Each of us has the capacity to reach or attain something bigger than ourselves, bigger than our tendency to quit and take flight. At some point, we too must find what causes a shift so powerful inside us that we break the habit of fleeing and decide to stay the course as we grow in wholeness and fulfillment.

So what does this have to do with my dad refusing to allow me to quit the football team? He modeled for me what it took to instill perseverance in another. First, my dad called me to a core value that guided our family: *Finish what you start.*

Part of our responsibility as parents is to instill foundational life principles into our children. This does not happen by osmosis, but by speaking, modeling, and expecting these principles to guide their lives as they guide our own. In every way, positively or negatively, a parent helps define the culture of a family, no matter what sort of family it is. That influence can be a positive or negative one, depending on the parent's character, presence, and faith—or lack thereof.

In 2 Timothy 2:2, Paul encourages Timothy, his spiritual son, to reproduce in others what he had produced in him, "You have heard me teach things that have been confirmed by many reliable witnesses. Now teach these truths to other trustworthy people who will be able to pass them on to others" (NLT). Paul deemed certain principles important enough to instill them in Timothy and make certain they were passed along to others. My dad was the same way.

As I have reflected on people who have had great influence on my life, without exception they have been people with foundational values and principles that guided their lives. Covey states that such values are like compasses that point the way and "if we know how to read them, we won't get lost, confused, or fooled by conflicting voices and values" (Covey 1990, 19). This settled sense of direction within a person's life is desperately needed today when so many conflicting voices and values call out to us.

AN ORGANIZATION'S CULTURE IS CREATED NOT BY WORDS WRITTEN, BUT BY VALUES THAT ARE EXERCISED DAILY.

My father did this on multiple occasions and in multiple ways. In reality, that is the underlying reason I wrote this book. I wanted to pass down to my sons the values and truths that their grandfather passed down to me. Values are not like DNA that one generation automatically gives to another. It is an intentional process. These values must be spoken, modeled, and then internalized over time.

Leaders do this in organizations and teams as they intentionally create a culture that is based on values they deem valuable and foundational for the greater whole. Furthermore, the culture is created not by words written, but by values that are exercised daily. I tell my students all the time, culture is not determined by a written mission statement, but rather by actions lived out consistently that reinforce the intentioned values. We have all read beautifully written mission statements that turn out to be just words on a wall or page. On the contrary, by not allowing me to quit football, my dad was reinforcing a value that he deemed worthy enough to instill in my life. His actions demonstrated that his son must finish what he starts.

Second, my father walked alongside me as we lived out perseverance and restoration together. Notice what my father did. He not only drove me to the gym; he then stood alongside me as I spoke to the coach that morning. In essence, his actions would not let me quit. And when humble pie had to be eaten, he was right there beside me. I must admit that his faith in me was always greater than my own, so his admonishment and his example of accountability always called me to a higher standard. If he had not, then perhaps my life would have been littered with the debris of being a quitter.

Interestingly, my dad's personal faith journey did not begin until he was forty years old. Baby Boomers remember Sunday evening church services. It was in one of those services that my father made a decision to follow Christ. There was no sermon shared or "invitation" given. The Holy Spirit began to do a work in his heart. My dad and many others began standing and walking to the altar to confess their need for Jesus. An eleven-year-old boy, I sat and listened in amazement as my stoic father confessed his need for Christ.

After that night, my father's life was different in so many ways. He began to be guided by the principles and values of his faith. He began to teach a Sunday School class, getting up in the predawn hours every Sunday to study the Bible and prepare to teach that morning. This continued for over fifteen years. In some ways, my dad hid his emotions before that night. Afterwards, he began to speak openly about his affection for my mom and for us, his children. My brother, sister and I remember that before that night, Dad rarely hugged us or told us he loved us. After that night, we couldn't get away from him! We never said good-bye without him placing his arms around us, kissing us on the cheek, and telling us he loved us and how proud he was of us.

Following that decision, his faith began to define the culture of our home. Dad's faith was not an overbearing, legalistic thing. His faith was sincere, understanding, gracious, and compassionate. He made certain we understood that honesty, respect, courtesy, and hard work were values important to our family. Those values were expressed in certain behaviors, such as finishing what we start.

The morning Dad walked into the gym beside me was just more evidence of the values he held. When we arrived at the gym that morning, Dad didn't say a word. His presence gave me the strength and resolve to overcome my fear and do what needed to be done. Bottom line, I knew Dad was there for me.

Many organizations and groups espouse values right and left, but fail miserably at walking alongside their people while those values are being taught and caught. Ecclesiastes 4:9–12 says, "Two people are better off than one, for they can help each other succeed. If one person falls, the other can reach out and help. But someone who falls alone is in real trouble. Likewise, two people lying close together can keep each other warm. But how can one be warm alone? A person standing alone can be attacked and defeated, but two can stand back-to-back and conquer. Three are even better, for a triple-braided cord is not easily broken" (NLT).

This passage reminds us that all of us need someone to be there for us. There is strength in numbers, and it is easier to get up from failure if someone is there to help us up. Not everyone has someone in their corner. This is particularly true if their family and friends have not seen anyone model how to walk alongside another. Organizations, businesses, and teams that do this well harness the energy, courage, and strength of their members. Those that don't lose valuable people along the way.

I am certain my dad would have desired to be somewhere else that morning. Watching your son eat crow and grovel at 6:30 A.M. probably wasn't on his Top Five to-do list. Yet there he was, standing with me while I worked through my mistake. At that moment, I knew how much he cared about me. And each night for two weeks when I came home from practice, after running my imposed penalty of an extra fifteen 100-yard belly slams, my dad would tell me I was doing the right thing and that he was proud of me. You see, walking alongside another not only imparts strength but also the encouragement needed to take another step. (Or, in my case, to run another 100 yards!)

What he did offers multiple lessons for those of us who influence and lead others. First, as persons of influence, we can enable others to stay the course by our admonishment, encouragement, and expectations. This models for others the values that give our tribe or organization meaning and direction. By constantly lifting up those values so that everyone hears and sees them, we give a clarion call to what will guide and define us.

Many say the most important thing Winston Churchill brought to England during wartime was his commitment to "never give in." During that time, Churchill was asked to speak at Harrow School (Churchhill 2003, 306–307). When it came time for his speech, he walked to the podium and said, "Never give in. Never give in. Never, never, never, never — in nothing, great or small, large or petty — never give in, except to convictions of honor and good sense." Churchill had more to say, but these words were remembered because he modeled them. Churchill's continual presence, persistence, and encouragement enabled a nation to rise to challenges which would have caused others to surrender. Sometimes a leader's persistence and insistence enables insistence and persistence to be lived out in others.

Second, it is crucial that leaders remember people are stronger together. Too many times, leaders call forth great values for people to follow, but never give them the support or vehicles necessary to come on board. Have you ever noticed it would be extremely hard to get on an Interstate highway without an on-ramp? The same can be said for organizations that don't understand the truth that people need to learn, model and experience culture in order to own the culture.

Leaders who know how to walk alongside their people and how to enable them to walk alongside each other are much more effective at developing and keeping the right people. My dad did these things for me and we can do them for others. It worked for Peter as he stepped out of the boat and it worked for Churchill as he led his country through war. It can also work for us as we challenge one of the worst decisions of a person's life, quitting.

Discussion Questions

1. Are you contemplating quitting a difficult commitment or fleeing from a struggle in your life right now?
2. What issues are causing you to panic? What do you fear?
3. What steps do you need to take, as an individual or as a team, to face your obstacles and finish what you have started?
4. To whom can you go to for advice, admonishment, support, and encouragement?
5. With whom will you covenant to share this journey?

Do the Right Thing, Even When It Costs You

The Power of Integrity

MY FATHER SERVED ON THE LOCAL SCHOOL BOARD FOR OVER FIFTEEN years. It was a rather thankless job, but one my dad took very seriously. He deeply believed in education and worked hard to support our schools in any way possible. Sometimes the job became extremely difficult when tough decisions had to be made.

On one particular occasion, a teacher was dismissed because of poor personal choices. When word got out that this person's contract would not be renewed, our phone began to ring off the hook. The phone calls were not to congratulate or thank my father for making the right and difficult decision, but to berate him and curse him. A few callers even threatened him.

I was a junior in high school when this happened and participated in the program this teacher gave leadership to. When I heard the news, I too was angry. All of my classmates knew my dad was on the school board and therefore knew he helped make this decision. So I went home and expressed my anger and frustration to my dad. I also shared the fact that his decision had placed me in a very uncomfortable position. With that, I stalked to my bedroom to huff and puff some more.

After a while, my dad came back to my room and shared quietly that the right choice had been made. He never shared any details, but explained that there were extenuating circumstances and he had no doubt the right decision was made. After hearing this, I came to believe that the right decision had indeed been made. The rest of the evening, I watched and listened to my dad personally take every angry phone call. He did not try to explain everything to everyone. He would just simply say the right decision had been made and he would stick by it and support it.

I finally asked him why he continued to serve on the school board. The pay was minimal to say the least and the headaches came by the bundle. Why would anyone want to deal with what he was dealing with, especially tonight? He looked at me for a moment and said, "Sometimes responsibility is not easy and difficult decisions have to be made. But when you know in your heart that decision is right, then you do the right thing, even when it costs you."

I loved and admired my dad, especially that night. I had seen him turn down jobs from those who wanted to give him substantial work if he would lie about insurance coverage. My dad would look them in the eye and say, "Daniels Roofing doesn't do business like that." On our farms we had some timber that had to be cut. One man told my dad he would cut the timber for a certain price and pay my dad "a bonus" in cash, so he wouldn't have to pay the income taxes on it. My dad firmly replied, "I don't do business like that and you won't be cutting our timber."

All my life, I witnessed my dad making difficult decisions, even when they cost him. But unbeknownst to him, I had a decision to make that night. I had not shared with my dad that some of my classmates were going to stage a boycott from classes the next morning because of the teacher's firing. The group had agreed to meet at the school office the next morning and, after making their case known, would walk out together. I now understood that we were planning an emotional but wrong response. So how should I handle it?

Most of my friends were in favor of the boycott as I had been before learning the truth. After contemplating this most of the evening, I finally told my mom and dad I had to go out for a little while. It was already late for a school night, so my parents protested. I simply looked at my dad and said, "This is important. You've got to believe me and trust me right now." And with that he said, "OK." I think he understood more than he acknowledged.

I had called some of my friends who were organizing the boycott and asked them to meet me. They all came, and I explained that the whole story of the teacher's situation had not been shared. In light of this, I said the boycott was the wrong thing to do and that we had to help stop it. They all agreed.

The next morning, we met at school early. One by one, as students made their way to the school office, we talked with them and shared why the boycott was wrong. We suggested the best thing to do was to go to class and let other people handle this.

Some disagreed and were angry that we were not going to do it; but most listened and agreed that the boycott should not happen. My dad had heard what had happened when he arrived home from work. He came to my room and said, "You and your friends headed off something that could have been very bad. I'm really proud of you for taking a stand."

The truth is, I was just copying what I had seen modeled the night before, what I had seen from a lifetime of being around this man. Jesus challenges us to "let your yes be yes and your no be no" (Matt. 5:37, NIV). He charges us to live a life of honesty and integrity, even if the right thing costs us. My dad modeled this for me on a continual basis.

If one leads long enough, there will be times when difficult decisions must be made, whether as a parent, teacher, team leader, or CEO. In some of these moments, the decision could cause great turmoil and angst. Lifetime friends could walk away, innuendos and lies could color one's reputation, while critics' ridicule and slander could affect one's family. However, none of those things diminish the joy of looking in the mirror and knowing that the right action was taken in the right way.

In those situations, it is best to model my dad's example: Don't try to defend yourself but allow your yes to be yes and your no to be no. I have a deep conviction that truth and integrity win out over time. Truth is like an air bubble trapped under water; it eventually makes its way to the surface. Also, we understand that truth may not always be exposed in this life; but at some point, each of us will be held accountable to the greatest Truth Teller, and right will be made known.

We live in a compromising world. Compromise is the right thing to do if each party will give some so that the greater good may be obtained. However, at times compromise means giving up your integrity by betraying your responsibility to others. That's when you must determine whether you will take the right step, knowing there will be a cost. It will never be the easy choice, but it will almost always be the right choice.

SOMETHING DEEP INSIDE US BEGINS TO ERODE WHEN WE DO NOT STAND UP FOR THE THINGS THAT MATTER MOST.

Martin Luther King, Jr. once said, "Our lives begin to end the day we become silent about the things that matter" (Chickering et al. 2006, 243). Something deep inside us begins to erode when we do not stand up for the things that matter most. The initial decision may seem simple enough; but as time passes, we must turn a deaf ear or close our eyes to other situations we know are wrong. The erosion of our soul eventually reaches the point where we are but a shell of the person we once were.

Sometimes doing the right thing is not about standing against wrong, but about how we respond to the wrong done to us. The story of Joseph in the Bible is a perfect example of this. Let me give you Joseph's life in a nutshell. He was born into a life of wealth and was one of twelve sons. In fact, he was the favorite son. Genesis 37 informs us that Joseph's father loved him more than all the other sons. No wonder the text also informs us that his brothers despised him.

Finally, Joseph was sent to give a message to his brothers in the field. As they viewed Joseph coming from a distance, they decided to exact revenge on Joseph's arrogance. They threw him in a cistern and later sold him as a slave. He was taken to Egypt and sold to a man named Potiphar, who later placed him in prison for being falsely accused by Potiphar's wife.

Joseph was imprisoned for years. There came a time when Pharaoh had some dreams that nobody could discern. A man who had met Joseph in prison remembered that he had the capacity to interpret dreams and informed Pharaoh of this. Joseph was summoned from the prison and brought into Pharaoh's presence, where he interprets the monarch's dream about seven years of blessing and the seven years of famine. Pharaoh said, "Can we find anyone else like this man?" (NLT). So he took Joseph from being a prisoner and put him over all of Egypt, second in command only to him. Joseph became the governor of Egypt. Notice the journey his life took—favored son, hated brother, prisoner, slave, and then governor of Egypt.

Talk about a roller-coaster ride of life and a person who had every reason to be bitter! Instead of holding grudges against his brothers, Joseph chose to move forward and leave his hurt and hate behind. Joseph choose to respond to wrong in the right way, even though the wrong had cost him greatly. In truth, our healing and restoration will ultimately be determined by our decision to move past our hurt and our hate toward wholeness.

Isaiah 43:18–19 says, "Forget the former things; do not dwell on the past. See, I am doing a new thing! Now it springs up; do you not perceive it? I am making a way in the desert and streams in the wasteland."

If you and I ever want to abandon a victim mentality and not allow it to dominate our hearts, then at some point we must find the capacity to forget and forgive the events that have hurt us for too long. Like Joseph, we will have to cultivate a willingness to forgive.

I say "cultivate" for this reason: I don't think forgiveness is a natural response for most of us, especially when we have been wronged. It's easier to hang onto our bitterness instead of paying the cost of forgiveness. You see, if we choose forgiveness, we forego the opportunity to get even. It also costs us to give up the burden of old anger. Forgiveness is about weighing the costs and doing the right thing when it would be easier to continue carrying our hurt.

Genesis 50 recounts the moment when Joseph chose to do the right thing: "But now that their father was dead, Joseph's brothers became fearful. 'Now Joseph will show his anger and pay us back for all the wrong we did to him,' they said. So, they sent this message to Joseph: 'Before your father died, he instructed us to say to you: "Please forgive your brothers for the great wrong they did to you—for their sin in treating you so cruelly." So we, the servants of the God of your father, beg you to forgive our sin.' When Joseph received the message, he broke down and wept.

"Then his brothers came and threw themselves down before Joseph. 'Look, we are your slaves!' they said. But Joseph replied, 'Don't be afraid of me. Am I God, that I can punish you? You intended to harm me, but God intended it all for good. He brought me to this position so I could save the lives of many people. No, don't be afraid. I will continue to take care of you and your children.'" (vv. 15–21, NLT)

Notice that Joseph not only chose to forgive his brothers but to take care of his brothers and their children. Doing the right thing regarding how we respond to wrong is not only about releasing ourselves from the hurt of the past, but also releasing others from their part of the hurt. The cost of responding to wrongs committed against us is to share the unmerited grace that Jesus gave to us. "Instead, be kind to each other, tenderhearted, forgiving one another, just as God through Christ has forgiven you" (Eph. 4:32 NLT).

Amy Rees Anderson (*Forbes/Entrepreneurs*, Dec 6, 2012, 1–3) tells the story of walking along a street on the way to a business dinner with a wonderful gentleman named Buddy; one of her clients at the time. As Buddy and she walked along the street, a stranger walked up to them and asked if they could give him some money. She paused for a moment, thinking to herself, "Is it safe to give this man money, or is he a scam artist?" While she was still contemplating how she should react to the situation, Buddy responded by pulling out a $20 bill and handing it to the man.

After the stranger thanked him and walked away, Amy started to explain to Buddy that she had been uncertain of whether it was safe to give the man money. Buddy said, "I would rather be made a fool for helping a man who wasn't in need, than to be made a fool for not helping a man who was."

That comment changed Amy's life. Buddy was right: We ought to be the kind of persons who make every attempt to help those in need. In that moment, Amy committed to never again hesitate when it came to doing the right thing.

Amy says she no longer makes a decision in the heat of the moment because she has made that decision in advance. She knows that if we pause to decide, we will either talk ourselves out of helping or start justifying all the reasons that we don't need to help. By making her decision to help ahead of time, she no longer has to think about it at all. She simply has time to react and do the right thing.

Brook Jones (Jones 2016) agrees that keeping a few simple scenarios in mind makes living easier. She offers these specifically:

If I see a person in need...do the right thing.
If I have an opportunity to get ahead, but it is at
the expense of others...do the right thing.
If I did someone wrong and need to
apologize...do the right the thing.

Now I'll offer a few additional scenarios.

If I have the opportunity to speak truth, but a
lie would be easier...do the right thing.
If I have the opportunity to do right, but it might
upset some people...do the right thing.

**If I see a person being ridiculed and I could
join in…do the right thing.
If I hear gossip and could perpetuate it…do the right thing.
If I have been hurt and could offer
forgiveness…do the right thing.**

An advance commitment to do the right thing enables us to act rightly, despite the cost. Les Parrot shares a story by Denis Waitley about a rookie nurse's first day on the job. She was to join the surgical team at a large, well-known hospital and we can all imagine the pressure associated with that day. One of her responsibilities in the operating room was to ensure that all instruments and materials were accounted for at the end of the surgery. During her first surgery, as the surgeon prepared to close the incision, she said to him, "You've only removed eleven sponges, and we need to find the last one."

"I removed them all," declared the doctor emphatically. "We'll close the incision now."

"No," the rookie nurse objected, "we used twelve sponges."

"I'll take the responsibility," the surgeon said grimly. "Suture."

"You can't do that, sir," blazed the nurse. "Think about the patient."

The surgeon smiled, lifted his foot, and showed the nurse the twelfth sponge. "You'll do just fine in this or any other hospital" (Parrott 2007, 197).

That was the kind of integrity passed down to me by my father. He was a kind and gentle man, but his resolve to do the right thing was of heroic proportions. His life taught me that leadership is not always about placating people or taking the easy way out. Sometimes, our values and convictions call for us to do the right thing, even when there is a cost. If we live with the inner commitment to do the right thing when the storms come—and over time, storms come to all of us—that foundational principle will be an anchor that secures us, regardless of the cost.

Discussion Questions

1. Is there a part of your life that is compromised right now?
2. Is the compromise causing you to lose a part of yourself?
3. How have you pondered certain decisions in your life to prepare you for such situations?
4. After seeking the advice of others, what steps will you take to make changes?
5. What foundational values and principles will guide your decision about this matter?

CHAPTER

Don't Just Settle

The Power of Seeking God's Best

I WAS HOME FROM COLLEGE FOR THE SUMMER BREAK. FOR TWO PREVIOUS years, I had been in a very serious dating relationship with a young woman who was beautiful, bright, and articulate. Moreover, she shared my spiritual beliefs. There was only one problem. We had frequent disagreements and many of those disagreements ended in heated exchanges. Those moments left us more frustrated than words can say. But I never did anything about the situation, nor did I say anything to anyone, especially my parents, regarding the matter. I just kept moving down the same dysfunctional relational path.

On a warm summer evening, we had one of those heated exchanges. This one, however, was a little different in that it happened right outside my parent's home. Plus, it was very vocal for all to hear as the anger rose in our voices. As was the case in many of these confrontations, she drove away in a huff.

I just stood in our driveway, trying to figure out what had gone wrong again. Then I heard our front door open and saw my dad walking out toward me. To be very honest, it was the last thing I wanted to have happen at that moment. I was frustrated and embarrassed enough and had no desire to discuss the matter further. Dad simply stopped and asked if I was OK. I said yes and tried to cover over what I knew everyone in our home had just heard.

After a moment, he said, "Son, you know I have never been one to pry into your love life. But tonight, I feel like I have to say some things, so bear with me. I've noticed you and Brenda (not her real name) spend a great deal of time arguing and that anger between the two of you has become a real issue."

I began to defend her, but Dad interrupted. "Rolland, just give me a moment and listen to what I have to say. Your mother was not the only woman I ever dated. There were other girls. Eventually, though, everyone has to decide if someone they're dating is the person they want to spend the rest of their life with. My question to you is this: Do you really want to keep going through what you are currently going through with Brenda? Do you want to live with the drama and the struggle of trying to get along?"

He continued, "From what I see, I think the answer is no. And if you think this through, I think you will agree. It's hard to see much joy for either one of you right now.

"Son, you may settle for certain things in life. You may settle for one car over another or even one job over another for a while. But never settle for a spouse that you do not believe is God's best for you. Do me a favor and think hard about that, because that choice will determine your happiness for the rest of your life."

With those words, Dad walked away. At that moment, I was reminded of God's promise for us in Jeremiah 29:11: "For I know the plans I have for you," declares the LORD, "plans to prosper you and not to harm you, plans to give you hope and a future."

Too many times, people do not experience that hope and blessing in their future because they settle for what is not God's best for them. They do not have a person like my dad who would speak truth to them in love.

Needless to say, a few months later, Brenda and I broke up. It was the best decision for both of us. Brenda went on to marry a wonderful man and I understand they are very happy.

You may ask why I waited a few months to make the decision. The truth is, I was stubborn and wanted to make what was not best seem like God's best. However, my dad's words stayed with me and finally I had the courage to act.

Some years later, God brought to me his best in my wife, Ellen. I cannot imagine my life without her and cannot fathom this life without sharing the love we do. We both realize that we have been given a special love and we work very hard not to take it for granted or allow it to diminish in any way. At times I simply look at her and think of all I would have missed had I settled for another. I have great clarity regarding the importance of my dad's insight that day. It was the catalyst that moved me to pursue and wait for God's best.

I want to encourage you to assess your life and ask this question: In what areas of your life have you been willing to settle? Do any of them include major decisions that should have been non-negotiable areas of God's best for you? If so, you are likely to know disappointment and discouragement, not hope and prosperity.

I do not mean prosperity simply in terms of financial means. Here prosperity has to do with every area of your earthly life. Your emotional prosperity, your relational prosperity, your physical prosperity, and your spiritual prosperity are all a part of this equation. This prosperity speaks to the wholeness, contentment, and fulfillment of your life. Every aspect of your life will be affected if you settle for less than what you know to be God's best for you.

Sometimes moving toward God's best involves overcoming our embarrassment and even swallowing our pride. It may mean facing up to a history of poor decisions and acknowledging that we need help in doing the right thing instead of settling as we have so many times before. Not settling may mean drastic changes if you are bogged down in comfort or routine. It may mean Christian counseling to help you deal with emotional baggage that continually weighs you down and causes you to make poor decisions time after time.

Many times, it will mean overcoming the destructive voices of the past that have long told you that you don't deserve any better. Perhaps you have never been told that God has a hope and a future for you. Some people have been led to believe that their past will always determine their present and their future. The words *hope* and *future* are as foreign to them as the language of another country. They have never had another person like my dad to encourage them not to settle. In fact, if they're really honest, settling may even have been part of the legacy passed down to them by their family and others.

If this is true for you, then heed the wisdom of Rick Warren's words: "We are products of our past, but we don't have to be prisoners of it" (Warren 2002, 37). Please allow me to speak truth to you as my father did to me. Someone wishes more for you than you could wish for yourself. Just as my dad loved me too much to remain silent while I went my misguided way, so does God. Psalm 37:3-4 instructs us to "Trust in the LORD and do good. Then you will live safely in the land and prosper. Take delight in the LORD, and he will give you your heart's desires" (NLT). Perhaps it is time for you to take hold of the fact that Someone does love you and desires to give you a hope and a future.

You may have been quick to settle for second best because you have a hard time believing you deserve God's best. Your brokenness or shattered confidence may feed insecure self-doubt within you. Instead of expecting good, you expect impending failure. The fear for some is so great that settling for second-best, or even third best, always seems better than what they deserve. These persons don't really see this as settling; they are just content with anything better than the failure they see within themselves.

This dilemma reminds me of a story I once read about a man named Eisek, the son of Jekel. One night, Eisek dreamed that he was summoned to travel to far off Prague, the capital of Bohemia. There he was to dig for a hidden treasure that was buried beneath the large bridge which led to the castle of the Bohemian king.

At first Eisek just ignored the dream, but it kept recurring, so he took courage and set off for Prague. When Eisek finally reached the bridge, he discovered it was guarded day and night by the Bohemian king's finest guards. All Eisek could do was to come daily to the bridge and look over its side, staring at the spot where the treasure was supposed to be buried. Eventually, the captain of the guards asked

Eisek why he came to the bridge every day. When Eisek told the guard the whole story, he just rolled with laughter.

"You poor old ignorant man," the guard said, "No sane person would trust such stupid dreams! Why, if I were so stupid as to act on my dreams I would go to Poland, to Krakow in fact, and there dig for treasure in the dirt behind the stove in the home of one named Eisek, son of Jekel. I suppose half the men in Poland are named Eisek and the other half Jekel! Now, wouldn't that be the most stupid thing to do in all the world?" Eisek thanked the man for his advice and hurried home. And there, in a neglected corner of his own home, he discovered the treasure that put an end to all his misery (Johnson 2003, 301–302).

This simple story contains some important truths. First, inside each one of us God has placed a treasure of potential. In fact, Jesus informs us that he came so that we might have wholeness and fullness as we discover His treasure in this life. In John 10:10, Jesus said, "My purpose is to give them a rich and satisfying life" (NLT).

> GREAT POTENTIAL IS NEVER REACHED ON
> THE SHORELINE, BUT ONLY AS WE MAKE OUR
> WAY TO THE DEEPER WATERS OF FAITH.

Believe it or not, you were created for this fullness and wholeness. But please notice something else about Eisek's story. Eisek came to discover his treasure only after he would not accept his present circumstances or settle for how others perceived his pursuit of a dream. His dream found reality only after he risked failure in order to pursue it.

The second truth we find in the story of Eisek is the importance of stepping out in faith to pursue God's best for your life. Great potential is never reached on the shoreline of faith; but only as we make our way to the deeper waters of faith. However, many people are completely averse to risk because of a bruised past and lingering self-doubt.

I can relate to this. My first-grade teacher, Mrs. Harbour, told my mom, "Rolland is such a perfectionist that instead of doing something wrong, he just won't do it." Remember, that was in the first grade!

For too long, failure was something I avoided at all cost. Eventually, I learned that most of the great and wonderful things of life could not be accomplished or experienced without some possibility of failure. Then I began to give myself permission to fail and ventured out where failure was always a possible outcome. I discovered that failing did not mean that I was a failure.

Erma Bombeck, noted newspaper columnist and speaker, was asked to speak at a college commencement. She told the graduates, "I have been asked to stand before you and speak, not because of my accomplishments, but because of my failures. Allow me to share a few: I once had a comedy album that sold two copies in Beirut, a television sitcom that lasted about as long as a doughnut in our house, a Broadway play that never went to Broadway, book signings where I attracted two people, one who wanted directions to the restroom and the other who wanted to buy the desk at which I was sitting."

She concluded with these words, "You must always tell yourself, 'I am not a failure; I have only failed at something'" (Bombeck 2019).

Notice that last sentence: "You must always tell yourself 'I am not a failure; I have only failed at something.'"

Allow me to share with you three vital things regarding failure:

1. Failure happens to everyone.
2. You have the choice to view failure in one of two ways: either as a building block or a stumbling block. Choose the first option.
3. Failure is not an end, only the beginning to something better. The greatest mistake people make is seeing failure as an end. Failure is an end only if we allow it to be.

God the Creator has placed within each of us the potential of a great and wonderful future. But for that to come to fruition, we must not be willing to settle due to our fear of failure. At some point, we must risk failure in order to find all the good that God has in store for us, just as Eisek did in finding his treasure!

Our third truth from the Eisek story: All of us must work to develop our full potential. Eisek put forth the effort necessary to discover his treasure. He had to leave the comforts of home and journey to another country, facing unknown adversity in order to find that treasure. Treasure rarely just comes to us. It is the same with our innate potential. Neglected potential never develops into the greatness it can be; it always remains potential. You see, great potential without great effort is a great waste.

There is only one way potential is ever reached, through great effort. I was slow to catch on to this fact. I was blessed with the academic ability to coast and just get by. In high school, I knew the GPA I needed to stay academically eligible for sports, so I lived at that level. That was until the day I was called out in American History.

We had taken a test the day before and Mr. Edwards, our teacher, was walking around the room giving the graded exams back to each student without saying a word—until he got to me. When my test was laid on my desk, Mr. Edwards took two steps, turned around to face me, and said emphatically, "Mr. Daniels (he was always very proper), I believe you have it within you to do something special with your life, but at some point you must be willing to put forth the effort. You must stop just getting by." He looked down at me over the top of the glasses which were perched on the very end of his nose. Then he sighed and asked, "What do you have to say about that?"

Every head and body seemed to turn toward me. I remember at first being angry, then embarrassed, and I finally felt cornered. No one besides my parents had ever confronted me about my extreme academic laziness. I stammered through a few words, tried to be funny, and then just said, "You're right. I haven't given my best."

Mr. Edwards was a quiet and gracious man. He was a man I respected and at that moment I knew I had let him down. I stayed after class that day to talk with him. I am sorry the conversation happened during the last few weeks of my senior year because Mr. Edwards did not see the change I made academically. I was on the dean's list all through college and then earned more than a 3.9 GPA during both my masters and doctoral degrees. I share those facts not to brag, but rather to emphasize how one conversation can change a life. In so many ways, my conversation with Mr. Edwards did exactly that.

I learned that for a person to reach their full potential, they must be committed to hard work. Whether in your marriage, your vocation, or your parenting, you can achieve your best only by putting forth the necessary effort.

I called Mr. Edwards today, as I have periodically over the past forty-four years. This time, I learned that he had passed suddenly. I shared my story with his wife and she laughed, saying other students had told her similar things. I also wept with her on the phone because this iconic figure had passed from my life. Like my dad, he would not allow me to settle for mediocrity in a critical area of my life. I wish I had called him more often to tell him how much of an impact his words had on me and to share my appreciation for caring enough to call me out. He challenged me to move past my laziness to strive for my true potential.

Proverbs 20:4 says, "Those too lazy to plow in the right season will have no food at the harvest" (NLT). God has granted each of us a season of life, a season ripe with the potential of significance. But it is a season that will only bear a harvest if we are willing to till the soil, sow good seed, and put forth the effort necessary to grow our potential. It is a treasure of potential that we must risk to discover and pursue. This may require you to swallow your pride and change some decisions that have been less than God's best for your life, but you will never regret choosing God's best for you.

Will this always be an easy or simple choice? No. God's best always takes commitment, persistence, and work. It may not be easy, simple, or comfortable; but remember, great love is willing to languish in order to love well. God's best is not about easy or simple tasks; it is about loving much and loving deeply. It is not without thought of sacrifice, but with the intent to make any necessary sacrifice to grasp God's best.

It is the love we read about in Genesis 29, which describes how Uncle Laban required Jacob to work seven years for his daughter Rachel's hand in marriage. Verse 20 states, "So Jacob worked seven years to pay for Rachel. But his love for her was so strong that it seemed to him but a few days" (NLT). For Jacob, marital bliss was not a matter of settling but rather sacrificing what was necessary to obtain God's best for his life.

I simply close this chapter with this piece of advice: Never, ever, ever, ever, ever settle for less than God's best for you. If you have, then redirect your life and move toward what is best and right. Roll up your sleeves and do what is necessary to obtain God's best for you. That choice will be the difference between a future of hope or one of regret.

Discussion Questions

1. Are there areas of your life in which you have settled for something less than God's best for you?
2. What caused you to settle for that?
3. Are there skilled people (e.g., counselors or pastors) in your life who can help you deal with this situation?
4. What choices do you need to make to stop falling short of God's best for you?
5. Who will walk with you and support you as you make the necessary changes?

7 CHAPTER

Take Your Eyes Off of Yourself

The Power of Selflessness

I WAS A JUNIOR AT COLLEGE AND ATTENDED A WONDERFUL CHRISTIAN university. It was a small, private college located in the Midwest. In many ways, being there changed my life—that is, after the night I am about to share with you. You see, I was in a great place, surrounded by good people, and yet at that time something not so positive was happening inside me. I was becoming negative, critical, and cynical in my attitude toward my surroundings and life in general.

Every Tuesday night I would stand in the dorm hallway, wait for my turn on the hall phone, and then call my parents. (Some of us can remember those days gone by when cell phones were not in every pocket and purse.) After securing my parents on the line, I would begin what had become my normal routine of critical rhetoric: It would begin with complaints about classes, move to why I missed my girlfriend, worsened by being critical of those around me, and it would crescendo with some general complaints about life.

Finally, one night my dad had heard enough. He waited until my mom got off the other line and then spoke with great sternness. "Rolland, I want to say something before we hang up. I've heard enough of your complaining. I want you to do me a favor. I want you to get this chip off your shoulder. I don't know what has happened or is happening to you, but your outlook needs to change now. Get your eyes off the negative and quit feeling sorry for yourself. When you decide to do that, call me back. If and when you do, you are going to look around and realize that you are in a pretty good place. There are a lot of positive things and really good people all around you, if you will only recognize it. So do me a favor and please realize, life is just not that bad." With that, he hung up. He did not wait for a response and I felt fairly certain he did not care for one.

I stood there stunned, holding the phone in one hand and wondering what to do with what had just been given me. My father had corrected me many times during my childhood, but it had been many years since that type of pointed rebuke had taken place. He wanted to make a clear and certain point; and he had. In truth, it was a point that was long overdue.

I had become consumed with myself. The center of my universe was revolving around a single axis called Self. Everything in my thought process was in some way tethered to my world, my feelings, and my welfare. It was all about me, me, and me. I was viewing the world like a child, therefore Dad corrected me like one. In hindsight, I received exactly what I deserved and most assuredly what I needed.

I pouted for a while. Self-absorbed people have a tendency to do this. However, after some time passed, I began to honestly reflect on what my father had said. I began to awaken to the fact that things weren't nearly as difficult as I had previously imagined. The tunnel vision of self was filtering out the good and positive all around me.

Naaman was that way. In 2 Kings 5, Naaman is described in ways most people would envy. He was highly respected and admired, even by the king himself. When Naaman talked, people listened; where he walked, people watched. He held a very powerful position as commander of the king's army. He was a celebrity in his country and in his own mind. Because he was such an effective soldier, his name was associated with great battle victories and he was given the title of "mighty warrior."

On the outside looking in, one might say that Naaman lived a charmed life. We might look upon his life with great envy and wish we had it as good as Naaman did. However, in spite of his prestigious position and titles, there was more to Naaman's story than meets the eye. As we continue reading, we learn that four simple words overshadowed all the other great traits that defined the mighty warrior: "Naaman suffered from leprosy" (NLT).

Leprosy was a dreaded skin disease. Rest assured, those four words influenced every other aspect of Naaman's life. As Naaman's story progresses, we learn some important truths that apply to all of us. The first one is this: Everybody has problems and struggles.

Not one person reading this book is perfect. No matter what position, power, wealth, or degree you may hold, I'm sure you have struggles and problems. For some of us, our problems can distort all other aspects of our lives. The illness of leprosy did this to Namaan.

In a casual conversation, a young servant girl spoke of her desire for her master, Namaan, to meet the prophet Elisha and have him heal the disease. Upon hearing there might be a way to find healing, Naaman went with his horses, chariots, and great gifts to find Elisha and buy this favor.

Please know, Naaman had come in style and arrived to impress. His arrival would in no way suggest his problem. He made his way to Elisha's house and waited at the door for someone to celebrate his arrival. But Elisha sent a messenger out to him with this message: "Go and wash yourself seven times in the Jordan River. Then your skin will be restored, and you will be healed of your leprosy" (2 Kings 5:10 NLT).

Because of Elisha's lukewarm welcome, the great Naaman became angry and stalked away. He pouted just as I had done. Listen to his pouting words: "I thought he would certainly come out to meet me! I expected him to wave his hand over the leprosy and call on the name of the Lord his God and heal me! Aren't the rivers of Damascus, the Abana and the Pharpar, better than any of the rivers of Israel? Why shouldn't I wash in them and be healed?" (vv. 11–12). With those words, Naaman turned and went away in a rage.

Namaan was a great man and so he expected a great response. But Elisha didn't even come out on the porch. He didn't peek through the curtains to see who was at the door.

He simply sent a messenger out to meet him. For Namaan, this would not do. He expected some kind of exotic, spectacular ritual to come before his healing, something that was worthy a man of his stature. Elisha simply responded, "Go wash yourself seven times in the river and you'll be healed. Have a nice day." Instead of doing what the prophet asked of him, Naaman stormed off like a spoiled child because his pride and high self-esteem wouldn't allow him to do the common. Elisha understood that Naaman's greatest need was not his leprosy, but his pride and self-arrogance.

Left to himself, Namaan's pride would have caused him to miss a miracle, his miracle. But, lucky for Namaan, he had some truth-tellers in his camp. The text states that his officers reasoned with him. They told him what he didn't want to hear. These were men who had earned his trust by going to battle with him and wading through the trenches where life and death hung in the balance. "But his officers tried to reason with him and said, "Sir, if the prophet had told you to do something very difficult, wouldn't you have done it? So you should certainly obey him when he says simply, 'Go and wash and be cured!'" (v. 13 NLT)

If not for their intervention, Namaan's brokenness—physically and emotionally—would have remained. The same result can happen to any of us.

That brings us to the second truth from Namaan's story: Arrogance, self-centeredness, and pride can be our greatest hindrances to wholeness. Scripture makes this abundantly clear: "Human pride will be humbled, and human arrogance will be brought down" (Isa. 2:17 NLT). "Pride leads to disgrace, but with humility comes wisdom" (Prov. 11:2 NLT). "But those who exalt themselves will be humbled, and those who humble themselves will be exalted" (Matt. 3:12 NLT).

In essence, Namaan's officers are telling him to get over himself and not be too proud to do the humble things God asks you to do. It is a lesson for all of us because we all can be held captive by our pride and self-centeredness. So in response to their encouragement, Naaman surrendered his pride, went down to the Jordan River, and there dipped himself seven times, just as the man of God had instructed him. The Scriptures inform us that at that moment, his skin became as healthy as the skin of a young child. Namaan's willingness to swallow his pride and act in obedience led to his healing from leprosy.

ONE OF THE GREATEST GIFTS GOD GIVES US IS THE REALIZATION THAT LIFE IS BIGGER THAN US.

If we continue reading the story, we soon discover that was not Namaan's only healing that day. Naaman and his entire party went back to find Elisha, the man of God. They stood before him as Naaman declared, "Now I know that there is no God in all the world except in Israel" (v. 15). His declaration gives to us our final truth from the story: God's greatest concern for us is always the condition of our hearts.

I told a friend not long ago that one of the greatest gifts God ever gives us is when He finally allows us to understand that life is a bigger than us. When we finally move past our own ego and self-centered agenda, we catch a glimpse of the bigger picture that a life of faith brings to us. There is so much more to life than what the self allows us to view. If we are willing to take our eyes off of ourselves, then God's greater good will come into focus.

The Bible challenges us to do just that with these words, "Nothing should be done because of pride or thinking about yourself. Think of other people as more important than yourself. Do not always be thinking about your own plans only. Be happy to know what other people are doing" (Phil. 2:3–4, NLT).

The cocoon of self closes us off from a deeper understanding of happiness and fulfillment. In the same way a butterfly larva wraps itself in a cocoon, we can shrink-wrap ourselves in a narrow and shallow view. If you have seen the movie, *Shallow Hal*, you will better understand what I mean. Hal Larson is a superficial man obsessed with dating beautiful women, which prevents him from seeing the character and worth of other women. Hal asks a motivational speaker to hypnotize him so he will begin to see the inner beauty of women, regardless of their physical appearance. He then begins dating a woman who is not his stereo-typical type. This puzzles his closest friend, who has always known him to be self-centered and materialistic. He wonders whether Hal has really shed his selfish cocoon.

The cocoon of self prevents our true beauty from being released as well as hindering us from acknowledging the true beauty of others. Very few people consumed with self ever know the depth of compassion and sensitivity needed to release the person they were created to be. It is also very difficult for self-centered people to see the beauty of others except to serve their own egotistical goals.

However, when a person decides to wrestle free from self-centeredness, like a butterfly breaking out of its cocoon, a new world and new person are revealed. This person now sees a bigger picture of life, in which caring for and sharing with others transcend selfish motives. Joy and laughter characterize this person's life as joy and laughter are shared with others.

It is too easy to remain inwardly focused, especially when things are not going the way we wish they would. Namaan illustrates that. Such people strengthen their guard and become wary of others. The reasons are twofold. First, it takes less effort and energy to focus only on ourselves. Second, when we feel threatened, our instinct of self-preservation takes over. We retreat into our shells like turtles and try to protect ourselves.

But herein lies a great problem: The steps we think are most secure may actually cause us the most harm. When we crawl into our protective shells, we seal ourselves off from the very people that we need the most. All of us need to retreat now and then, but none of us were created to be totally self-sufficient. In the words of Reuben Welch, "We really do need each other." Or, as I like to say, "None of us were meant to be the Lone Ranger."

Surrounding ourselves with a protective cocoon or shell is a survival tactic, but it alienates us from the love and support we need to survive. Over time, as we are absorbed with self-preservation, unresolved anger and bitterness can dominate our emotions. These attitudes can take us to a dismal place. Eventually, we find ourselves isolated in the very small and critical world of "me."

We must understand that the rewards and benefits of life are so much smaller when our total investment is in ourselves. We know greater rewards and benefits when we invest our energies outside ourselves and allow others to invest in us. None of us can do this if life is simply all about me and our joy is solely determined by what happens solely to me.

I met Brad Sims when I was 18 years old and we both were attending a local community college. I was there playing baseball and Brad was playing tennis. It's funny to me that Brad, a city boy and I a country boy connected on such a deep level. But we did. As I got to know Brad and his story, his joy and exuberance simply amazed me. Over the years, Brad has amazed me even more. Let me share a brief summary of his life and I think you will see my point.

- Three months before his birth, his father left his mother. As you might imagine, this caused financial hardships for Brad and his family.
- At age three, Brad and his mom moved in with his grandparents. It was a new apartment and the land line to the phone had yet to be connected. One evening, Brad suffered his first asthma attack. His mom walked to the pay phone on the corner and called a doctor. On her way back, she was stabbed to death. The murder has remained unsolved till this day.
- At age six, a week before he started first grade, Brad's favorite person in his young world, his granddad, died of a massive heart attack. Brad's young mind had difficulty grasping why his father, mother, and granddad had all left him.
- Brad's neighborhood was not the best environment for a young man without many role models to follow. During junior high, Brad's decision-making leaned toward poor and terrible. In his words, "I was just not a good person."

- In high school, Brad's life was a mixture of both positive and negative. He began to make some new friends who introduced the concept of faith to him. However, the lure of old habits was too strong and his life fell more off course. This season of life put Brad's grandmother through very hard times while she tried to raise him alone. However, it was at the end of this time that something significant happened in Brad's life: Jesus touched his heart. In Brad's words, "It was the first time I had ever felt the Lord speaking to me and nudging my heart. I knew I was different. I knew God was working on me."

- At age 20, Brad was contacted by a family friend who told him his father, whom he still had never met, would be attending a funeral in his hometown. His response was one of fear and underlying angst, yet he wanted to meet this man who held the title of father. The times and location of the memorial service were made public and Brad found himself attending a funeral for a man he didn't know with the intent to meet the father he had never met. Brad waited in line until he stood before his dad and shook his hand. His father asked how he knew the deceased and what brought him there that day. Brad looked him in the eye and said, "My name is Bradley Eugene Walker Simms and I am your son." The next few moments were quiet and uncomfortable, yet this meeting turned out better than expected. His father and his father's wife welcomed Brad with open arms into their family in Houston, and for the next twenty-five years Brad shared a positive relationship with his dad and family until his father's passing.

- At age 24, Brad came home to find his grandmother dead on the floor. She had been the only constant in a life filled with deep struggle. She raised him, stood by him, held him when he hurt, and disciplined him when he should have done better. Brad said, "For the first time in my life, I was truly alone, and I felt the depth of that aloneness. I was lost and hurt more than ever before." Yet, in that moment of deep sadness, Brad felt the Lord say to him, "You are not alone." Crazy, isn't it? Brad's faith began to find traction in the midst of this unbelievably deep and painful loss.

- In Brad's early thirties, he became a youth counselor for his church. One evening he took some students to a state convention. On their way home, a drunk driver was going the wrong way on the Interstate and hit Brad's car head-on. One of the students in the car was killed and Brad was very seriously injured. It was a devastating night, but the horrible injuries Brad sustained had a life-changing impact. Mentally, physically, and emotionally, the pain was almost unbearable. Multiple surgeries followed. Brad began receiving cards and letters from friends and strangers alike, informing him that people were praying for him and that their love was reaching out to him. Brad said he began to heal as he received God's love from God's people. It was during this time that Brad's faith became the true anchor for his life.

- At age 35, Brad got married and he and his wife were blessed with two children. They are the joy and pride of his life. When the kids were three and four, Brad was diagnosed with testicular cancer. Further testing revealed that the cancer had spread to multiple areas and Brad was informed he probably had only a few months to live. However, the doctor informed him of an experimental chemotherapy that was available. Brad underwent the treatment and, many months later, he was declared cancer-free! Further surgery was necessary to repair damage as a result of the chemo. Sadly, Brad's marriage ended during this stressful season.

- In his fifties, Brad had to undergo heart by-pass surgery to repair two blocked valves and replace the aortic valve. During this time, his diabetes caused ulcers on both feet. Brad lost two toes and a quarter of his left foot in this five-year ordeal.

- At age 61, Brad was diagnosed with blockage of his carotid artery. His doctor informed him the location of the blockage was dangerous and the chance of his having a stroke during surgery was extremely high. After many prayers, Brad asked for the surgery. My wife and I drove all night to be there for the surgery. God was gracious and the surgery went better than the surgeon expected.

- Last year at age 62, Brad had to have a hip replaced. This was the second time to replace the joint, which had been injured in the previous auto accident. On the day before that surgery, I called to pray with Brad. I told him how sorry I was that he had to undergo yet another medical procedure. However, Brad was upbeat and positive, immediately telling me how quickly he would be released from the hospital after it was over. "Rol, I am not worried in the least," he said. "It's just one more step in an uphill battle. The Good Lord's got me and always has."

A short time after that, Brad shared a letter that included a section he titled, *What I Am Sure Of.* These are the principles that guide and hold him:

1. God is in control if I let Him.
2. There is nothing that God won't help me through.
3. Life is a journey, but God is a constant and never leaves me alone.
4. I have no fear, only my love and trust in God.
5. Death is the end of this life; but there is more life with the Father.
6. My whole life has been a series of miracles!
7. I am a blessed man!

If anyone had a reason to be bitter about life, it is Brad Sims, yet he declares himself blessed. His actions and attitude confirm that conviction. Now let's take a step back and remember what my dad strongly advised that evening in the dorm hallway. A synopsis would be this: *Realize your experience is not all about you. Get your eyes off yourself and quit feeling sorry for yourself. You are not alone in this world and what has happened to you has happened to others. Everyone has problems and struggles, so look beyond yourself and realize there is a bigger world awaiting you, a world where a lot of positive things and really good people surround you. That world needs you and, believe it or not, you need it. When you realize this, you will begin to see the beauty of that bigger world and the world will finally begin to see the real beauty in you.*

Just like a butterfly freeing itself from its cocoon, this requires some wrestling and tearing yourself free from toxic attitudes that bind you. But through your wrestling and reflection, a bigger picture will begin to emerge—the picture of a life that is bigger than you. At this moment, you will see that your life is so much larger than your self.

Discussion Questions

1. Do you see your life as revolving around you?
2. Have past events caused you to retreat into a protective shell?
3. Have you limited your investment in others and prevented them from investing themselves in you?
4. What healthy relationships would help you break out of your cocoon?
5. What areas of your life do you need to surrender to God?
6. Do you have truth tellers in your life? Do you need to cultivate some who can help you stay focused on the positive?

8

Never Say, "I and Me" When You Can Say, "We and Us"

The Power of We

AT THE END OF EVERY WORK WEEK, THE FOREMEN OF DANIELS' ROOFING Company would enter my dad or uncle's offices to report the hours they had worked as well as the work hours of employees they supervised. It was also a time to tell the company owners what had been accomplished on each job and what needed to be done the following week. This was one of my favorite times. The men would hang around for an extended period, bantering and laughing about the week gone by. It was not difficult to see the affection and appreciation my uncle and father had for those who worked for them. Those feelings were reciprocated by the men with regard to my father and uncle.

On one of those Fridays, I sat in my dad's office and reported on the work accomplished during my week. He listened to me just as he had listened to many others that evening. After everyone's time had been noted and paychecks received, we locked up the office and went to meet some of the men for coffee before going home.

As we drove to the coffee shop, my dad asked if I minded if he made a suggestion to me. I was curious to hear what he had to say, so he began, "I noticed something tonight as you reported your week. You used the words, *I* and *me* a lot. Let me make a suggestion: Never say, "I" and "me" when you can say, "we" and "us." It goes a long way to building other people up and encouraging a sense of team to those who work with you. It might also keep folks from thinking you are all about yourself. As a leader, that will matter a lot."

Over the intervening years, I have sat through many leadership conferences, trying to gain a better understanding of the dynamics of leadership, yet I doubt that any conference gave me greater insight into leadership than those words spoken by my dad. Great leaders have always understood this principle: There is more power in *we* than in *me*.

Nehemiah exemplified this as he undertook the task of rebuilding the wall that surrounded Jerusalem. The task was so difficult that Nehemiah prayed and fasted about it for over four months before approaching the king to ask permission to go. Upon his return to Jerusalem, he found the wall in shambles and the people living a desolate and fearful life.

Nehemiah spent three days in Jerusalem before telling anyone why he had come. The following verse contains the first words he spoke to the people of Jerusalem about the difficult task facing them. Notice the pronouns he used to describe their plight and what they needed to do to change that plight: "You see the bad situation *we* are in, that Jerusalem is desolate, and its gates burned by fire. Come, let *us* rebuild the wall of Jerusalem so that *we* will no longer be a reproach" (Neh. 2:17, italics added).

Without doubt, Nehemiah understood the principle that there is more power in *we* than in *me*. He would need many others to come alongside him to accomplish the great task God had laid before him. In verse 18, the people of Jerusalem responded to Nehemiah in a way that would have been music to any leader's ears: "Come, let *us* rebuild the wall." This leader's mindset made the impossible possible in the city of Jerusalem.

Over the years, I have seen how the power of *we* has been evident in various situations. I have also become very aware of how many times a leader uses the words *I* and *me* instead of *we* and *us*. Those who have a tendency to be self-centered are usually poor team players who fail to enlist the commitment of others. They may briefly accomplish something great; but over the long haul, they falter for lack of team participation.

Self-centered leaders seldom have what it takes to build a team. On the contrary, servant leaders who focus on *we* and *us* cultivate other leaders around them. They make certain others are an integral part of the team and have ownership of the task at hand. As a result, "we-type" leaders have the capacity to accomplish greater things than "me-type" leaders.

Robert Greenleaf's essay, "The Servant as Leader," focused on the leader's need to invest in and grow others. Greenleaf described himself as a lifelong student of organizations and how things got done. A 40-year career in management and organizational development with AT&T led Greenleaf "to challenge educational institutions and business organizations to consider their social and human obligation to develop leaders who seek to ultimately improve society in a collectivistic rather than an individualistic manner" (Boyum 2008, 4–5).

Greenleaf's writings marked a radical paradigm shift in the role and assignment of leaders. Today, a growing number of leaders are searching for some type of balance across the many dimensions of their lives. They are coming to see wholeness and spirituality as necessary ingredients for satisfaction and meaning in their lives. Like Greenleaf, they are asking, Isn't there something more I can give my life to, beyond me?

Greenleaf's servant leadership theory is built upon the "we" principle. It is practically lived out as servant leaders swallow pride and sacrifice ego for the good of the whole. They are more focused on people than simply productivity. Greenleaf notes that these leaders help move organizations from a heavy emphasis on production to where they need to be, "with a heavy emphasis on growing people" (Greenleaf 1991, 120).

Servant leaders empower those around them instead of using power to dominate them. They establish trust by being completely honest and open, keeping actions consistent with their values and showing trust in their followers (Yukl 2002, 404). The apostle Paul informs us that Jesus led in this manner. Philippians 2:3–8 describes how Jesus sacrificed Himself for the good of the whole and, by pouring Himself out and emptying Himself, modelled what it meant to be a servant leader.

Servant leaders must learn to follow Jesus' example of sacrifice. It entails saying no to our self-filled ego, living selflessly regarding others, and loving them as much as we love ourselves. In this process, a leader ceases to be self-centered and starts becoming other-centered. To understand Jesus' example as a leader, we must first know Him as servant who lived out His words, "The greatest among you will be your servant" (Matt. 23:11).

SERVANT LEADERS EMPOWER THOSE AROUND THEM INSTEAD OF USING POWER TO DOMINATE THEM.

Nehemiah understood that true leadership is all about sharing life's journey with others. It is about attempting something bigger than oneself and realizing that, to accomplish this great thing, one must motivate others to come alongside the leader. A servant leader is constantly challenging, lifting up, and celebrating others along the way.

In the end, leadership is about accomplishing together what could not have been accomplished alone. It is about intentionally celebrating success with those who helped make the victory possible. People who are only about *I* and *me* never experience leadership like this. They also never experience life at its best, when it is shared—both the ups and the downs—with others.

One of the most common occurrences in me-centered leadership is when a leader becomes the bottleneck to a growing organization. Exodus 18 describes how the great leader Moses found himself in that predicament. Moses created an administrative quagmire by setting up a system that required all of the Israelites' community issues and decisions to pass through him. Most of us as leaders have had our moments as bottlenecks. We own too much, control too much, and can't give up enough because we believe we are bigger and better than we really are. Fortunately for Moses, his father-in-law Jethro understood that there is more power in *we* than in *me*. Notice what he said: "The next day Moses took his seat to serve as judge for the people, and they stood around him from morning till evening. When his father-in-law saw all that Moses was doing for the people, he said, 'What is this you are doing for the people? Why do you sit alone as judge, while all these people stand around you from morning till evening?'" (Exod. 18:13–14, NIV).

Jethro's statement, "the people stood around Moses from morning till evening," is a critical insight into the problem at hand. Moses was the center of all that happened and all that did not happen at the very same time. While Moses worked, the people stood around. All productivity centered around one person. Finally, Jethro asked the crucial question, "Why do you sit alone as judge?"

Notice it took an outsider to see the inner dysfunction of what was going on. Moses had grown comfortable in the role and the people were simply doing what they had always done. Sometimes it is true that we can't see the forest for the trees or the trees for the forest. "This is how we have always done it" or "this is how I have always led" can be the roadblock that many leaders must move beyond. Notice the dynamics we find in this bottleneck situation:

- Moses was overworked, overwhelmed, and overbooked.
- The people were underserved and underused.
- The community was stagnant and stalled.
- What was common and comfortable was neither effective nor efficient.

Most of the time, we find these dynamics when leadership is the bottleneck to growth and productivity. To move beyond the bottleneck, a leader must learn how to become a multiplier of others' talents and energies, not the sole user of talents and energies. Otherwise, the organization will never outgrow the handprint of the current leader; therefore, it never moves beyond its current stagnation.

We see Moses take certain steps in order to become a multiplier of others. First, Moses got over his Messiah complex. "Moses answered him, 'Because the people come to me to seek God's will. Whenever they have a dispute, it is brought to me, and I decide between the parties and inform them of God's decrees and instructions'" (Exod. 18:15–16).

It's easy to understand why Moses came to see himself as the sole Deliverer of his people. Think about it: When he spoke, ten plagues fell upon Egypt. When he ascended the mountain, God spoke. When he waved his staff, great miracles were seen. Trust me, most of us would have had to work through more than a little Messiah complex after that! When we have functioned a certain way over a long period of time, it's difficult to change our way of doing things. Becoming a multiplier of other people's resources is a bigger step for some leaders than it is for others. Those who like to be in control hate to give up anything for fear that it won't be done in the "right" way. In truth, this means they are afraid it won't be done their way!

Moses had to move beyond himself and become a multiplying leader to fully live out the power of *we*. If not, the burden of leadership would have ultimately worn him down, as it does most me-centered leaders. The development of those around him would have been stymied.

It is the same for each of us and our organizations. At some point, we must realize the ultimate goal is to outgrow us. We are not the end-all; we do not have the capacity to know-it-all; nor do we have the energy to be a do-it-all. We are one vessel in need of other gifted vessels functioning effectively around us. Wise leadership always focuses on building and benefitting what has been entrusted to the leader's care. Sometimes, this means moving beyond the status quo and empowering others around us.

Second, Moses recognized his limitations. "Moses' father-in-law replied, 'What you are doing is not good. You and these people who come to you will only wear yourselves out. The work is too heavy for you; you cannot handle it alone'" (Exod. 18:17–18).

Every leader knows someone who has problems, burdens, and disputes because all leaders do! Like Moses, they know firsthand that no one leader is gifted, called, and equipped to handle every issue that presents itself. Some of us find this difficult because we pride ourselves on being "answer people." We think our role is to be the one our people look to for a definitive answer or solution to any question or problem. We like this because, when people come to us, we feel needed and valued.

Ponder this for a while and watch the dynamics involved in your relationships with those around you. If you're a "me" person, you will come to realize this is really about your needs, not your people's needs. Over time, you have created a system that plays to your emotional need and grants you dysfunctional strokes as you solve other people's problems. Every great leader finally realizes that limitations are a normal part of life and every leader has them. In fact, the apostle Paul finally came to "boast" and "delight" in his weaknesses, because he felt more genuinely human as he admitted he had them. "But he said to me, 'My grace is sufficient for you, for my power is made perfect in weakness.' Therefore, I will boast all the more gladly about my weaknesses, so that Christ's power may rest on me. That is why, for Christ's sake, I delight in weaknesses, in insults, in hardships, in persecutions, in difficulties. For when I am weak, then I am strong" (2 Cor. 12:9–10).

There is a struggle involved with admitting our limitations and needs. Some of us fear that we might appear inept, weak, imperfect, and flawed when we do this. The truth is, we are all inept, weak, imperfect, and flawed... and worse! However, this is really good news since our weaknesses create an opening for the limitless power of Christ to be on display through us. Crazy to think about, isn't it? God can remove the poison of our human vanity only when we admit our weakness and total dependence on His ability to work through our weakness. We just have to love a God like that!

Moses' third step was to identify who would shoulder the burden. Jethro advised, "Select from all the people some capable, honest men who fear God and hate bribes. Appoint them as leaders over groups of one thousand, one hundred, fifty, and ten. They should always be available to solve the people's common disputes, but have them bring the major cases to you. Let the leaders decide the smaller matters themselves. They will help you carry the load, making the task easier for you" (Exod. 18:22–23).

In his classic book, *Good to Great,* Jim Collins wrote, "The executives who ignited the transformations from good to great did not first figure out where to drive the bus and then get people to take it there. No, they first got the right people on the bus (and the right people off the bus) and then figured out where to drive it. They said, in essence, 'Look, I don't really know where we should take this bus. But I know this much: if we get the right people on the bus, the right people in the right seats, and the wrong people off the bus, then we'll figure out how to take it some place great'" (Collins 2001, 41).

Becoming an effective multiplying leader ultimately depends on who we choose to pour our lives into and empower. Nehemiah's story reveals that he divided the Israelites into many different teams to accomplish the many and varied tasks called for. In fact, over forty individuals are named as leading specific aspects of the rebuilding. A few short months later, that decision to divide tasks had resulted in the impossible: The wall was completely rebuilt. In only fifty-two days, the people had come together and rebuilt a city wall that had been totally destroyed. Their success affirms the fact that defining the "who" and empowering the "who" are critical steps to accomplishing great things.

Never forget this principle: *Great accomplishments call for great participation.*

In 2016, the University of Connecticut Women's Basketball team won four national championships in a row, not simply because they had Brianna Stewart and Coach Geno Auriemma, but because they had a team that knew their individual roles but played together as a team. If you watched the game, you will remember one play that made this clear. It was when a walk-on senior guard named Briana Pulido hit a shot in the closing seconds, after the All-Americans had exited the game.

A play had been set up to give Pulido a chance to score. She was a pre-med student and walked on after a text from Stewart invited her to give playing on this team a chance. When Pulido took the shot and hit nothing but net, the whole bench erupted into a cheer of delirium. So caught up in the moment, Coach Auriemma left the bench area to embrace Pulido in a hug and then directed her back on the court to finish the game!

This moment demonstrated the dynamics that helped make UConn unbeatable over their previous seventy-five games. When asked about the secret to their success, Auriemma said, "There are three key ingredients that go into this kind of success; One, two, three," pointing to his three seniors. The three stars then went down the bench, hugging every member of the team. Great accomplishments always call for great participation.

If you are a leader or someday hope to be, remember that there is more power in *we* than in *me*. It is a critical leadership principle for any leader who desires to grow themselves and the people he/she has the privilege to lead. As servant leaders, we are called to share power, not hoard it. We are called to develop and grow those around us, remembering there is so much more to the people who work with us than their productivity.

In the end, with the right heart, the right people, and the right understanding of the power of *we*, great things truly can be accomplished.

Rolland E. Daniels

Discussion questions

1. Would people who have worked with you describe you as a *me* leader or a we leader? Why?
2. What steps do you need to take to become more of a *we* leader?
3. Who will you ask to hold you accountable to take these steps?
4. In six months, what task do you hope to accomplish and celebrate as a team?

9

I Have to Give You Up

The Power of Sacrifice

I HAD GRADUATED FROM COLLEGE AND RETURNED HOME TO WORK FOR MY uncle and father at the family-owned roofing company. The plan was for me eventually to take over the company that had been in our family for two generations. I would make the third. Over a period of three years, I had worked hard toward this end. In fact, the phrase "worked hard" might not even describe the exhaustion one can feel from the summer heat in Mississippi on a hot tar roof. But my dad had clarified what would be expected of me when I returned home upon my graduation: "Rolland, there is only one way to learn this business, and that is from the ground up," Dad said. "You'll probably work harder than any other college graduate." I don't know if that statement became true, but my dad and uncle certainly held to their end of the bargain!

However, in the midst of all that hard work, a struggle was going on inside me. I was constantly wrestling with the sense that God had something different for me to do with my life. Finally, very late one night I knew my decision needed to be made. I knelt beside my bed at 2 A.M. and surrendered my entire life to God. I promised I would do anything and go anywhere he called me to go. The next morning was

Sunday and I made my way to the little country church in Collinsville, Mississippi I had always called home. This was the church my great grandmother and grandmother helped to birth. In this wonderful little congregation people like Pete and Francis Brezeale, Earleen and Norwood Williamson, and Paul and Mary George made Christian faith a tangible reality.

It is important that Sister Ethel Frazier also be recognized as one of those influential people. (Down South at that time, we referred to our Christian elders as Sister or Brother So-and-So.) Sister Ethel was one of the first women preachers of our tribe. She was a prolific writer and poet. Even more important, I saw Jesus vividly in Sister Frazier's life as she cared for an invalid husband while living out her faith so consistently on a daily basis. Almost every Sunday, Sister Frazier would find me, place her hands on my shoulders, look me in the eye, and speak these words: "Rolland Daniels, God has His hand on your life. If you will let Him, He will use you one day." I could never escape her words or the sense that God's hand was somehow upon my life.

At the end of that particular morning worship service, I found myself at the altar and ended my searching for the past three years. I felt an amazing sense that God was affirming my decision to accept his call upon my life. I must admit that although Sister Frazier had died by that time, her words rang clear as I walked forward that day.

Something else happened that morning that had never happened before in my life. My mother came and prayed with me at the altar. Certainly, I had prayed with my mom many times, but she and Dad had always respected the altar as a very private and personal place for their children. "Besides," she always told me, "you might be there to pray about us!"

I began to say, "Mom, I need to tell you something," but she interrupted and said, "You don't have to tell me anything. I know you are going into the ministry."

I knelt there at the altar, stunned. She knew before I told her what had just taken place in my life. She was probably even more insightful into what this entailed. "Now, Rolland, you have to do the most difficult thing in your life," she said. "You have to tell your father."

She was right. I had to share with my dad the news of my decision at the altar, even though it had always been my dad's dream for me to come back and work with him. We had always been extremely close and the previous three years, as I worked alongside my uncle and him, had only strengthened our relationship. But now my decision would crush his dream and cause him great hurt.

I came home later that day and made my way to the bedroom where my dad was. I told him there was something I needed to share with him. We sat down on his bed and I began to describe my struggles over the past three years. I also stated that in recent months it had become clear to me that God had a different direction for my life. I then told him I would be leaving the company to prepare for the ministry. Dad didn't say a word in response. He just stood up and walked quietly out of the room. His seeming disappointment left me void.

At that time, I was working on a job that took me out of town each week, so I left the next morning without my father or I saying a word to each other. About two weeks later, he showed up in the town where I was working. He made his way up to the roof and asked if I could go "measure a roof" with him. That was my dad's way of saying he wanted to talk with me.

As we got into his car, my father hesitated a moment and then said, "Rolland, almost three years ago, the Lord shared with your mother and me that you would one day go into ministry. Believe it or not, we were both awakened by the same dream on the same night. That night we both had the sense that the Lord would call you into ministry. We knew that meant God would call you from this place. We believed this, but we couldn't make the decision for you. We had to wait for you to come to that decision yourself. But now I have to give you up. Truthfully, I had no idea it would be this hard, but today I am handing you over to the Lord. I also want you to know that I could never be prouder of you for what you have chosen to do with your life."

With those words, I saw my dad do something I've only seen him do twice in my life. He cried. It was a moment I will never forget. In fact, I am weeping as I write these words. But it was not only his emotions that moved me that day, but the powerful words of love he spoke to me: "I have to give you up."

Without doubt, these are some of the most difficult words any human being will ever say to someone they truly care about. Whether it is when we send our children off to college or the military, or when we release a loved one from suffering to pass on to eternity, giving up someone precious to us is neither easy nor simple. In doing that, we surrender not only our loved one but also a part of ourselves. Whether we're giving up our dreams, our security, or our comfort, we must let go of someone or something that is precious to us. Rest assured, this never takes place without sorrow.

In fact, the Bible refers to this as the act of dying. Jesus said, "For sure, I tell you, unless a seed falls into the ground and dies, it will only be a seed. If it dies, it will give much grain" (John 12:24, NLT).

When we surrender someone or something precious, a part of us dies. In many cases, it feels as though a vital organ has been torn away from us. Yet it is the only way to be faithful with what was given to us in the first place. The Bible is right: Such self-denial and selflessness may be the only way we can give another person the freedom and opportunity to fulfill God's will for them.

As I write these words, I am reminded of so many times when an individual had to surrender something without having a choice. I have sat with friends and family after a loved one has been tragically taken. I have gone to funeral homes with them to help plan a memorial service or choose a coffin. They would rather be anywhere else in the world because they had no choice in the matter.

However, we often do have a choice. Then we are called to do the bigger thing and see a bigger picture. Our action of giving up makes possible the greater good of another. If we choose to hold onto what we have, some good might still happen, but not the greater good that God has in store. This is true not only for individuals but for organizations as well. All of us have known leaders who held onto their positions too long and organizations that suffered because of their selfishness, fear, or unwillingness to move aside.

Power and position can become intoxicating and difficult to surrender. People convince themselves such a decision is not about them, but it is. Our need to be needed, to be in a position of power, or receive strokes of prestige can entice us to remain in place long after a change is necessary. We may convince ourselves that this is best when deep inside we know it is not.

We have all seen persons who refused to follow the selfless principal of giving up. What usually follows is a tale of hurt, perhaps even destruction. Tragically, these persons' refusal to release what they love brings great harm to their beloved.

The Bible is full of examples of people who gave up something or someone they loved for the sake of a greater good. Abraham did this with Isaac, the son of promise. Abraham had to give him up to God on Mount Moriah so that a nation might be born. Moses did this as he viewed the Promised Land, which he could never enter. After guiding the Israelites out to the bondage of Egypt, listening to their criticism, praying for their lack of faithfulness, and guiding them through the desert for forty long years, he gave them up to Joshua. In doing so, he freed them to experience the greater blessing God had in store for them.

God the Father did this ultimately with His Son, Jesus. John 3:16 informs us that "God loved the world so much that he gave his one and only Son, so that everyone who believes in Him will not perish but have eternal life" (NLT). The greater good called our heavenly Father to give up what was most precious to Him. That greater good also caused Jesus to say to the Father, "Not my will, but yours will be done" (Luke 22:42).

Many times, we are called to give up something we treasure. This is without doubt the highest and purest form of love.

This is a life principle that I have tried to model with our sons and other precious gifts God has given me. I have discovered that in giving up my blessing, I have received a greater blessing in return. Andrew Murray describes it this way: "The blessed receiving soon makes the giving up most blessed too" (Murray 1979, 51).

I know a man whose father did the exact opposite of mine. When this young man graduated high school, he had the opportunity to go away to college on a full scholarship. He had worked hard to earn this recognition. The scholarship was in his "sweet spot" and he was extremely excited about the opportunity. However, the young man's father would not allow him to accept it. He said he needed him to stay at home and help run the family business. The father saw his older son as the chosen one, while the younger one seemed to be the subject of constant criticism and emotional abuse.

The young man's heart was broken over this decision and his vision for a different life faded. You see, there is loss in giving someone up, but there is a deeper loss when selfishness will not allow someone to be given up. The young man did as his father wished and the result was painful to the son and ended up being extremely painful to the family.

The dysfunction that surrounded his home and workplace pulled him into a dark place. Over the years, dysfunction (which characterized other aspects of his life) continued to take a toll. The results destroyed his marriage and ultimately cost him the family business. His life spiraled even deeper into isolation and brokenness, while living with the ridicule of his father, who declared how right he had been not to allow his son to go away to college so that he could mess something else up.

Selflessness was never a part of this man's home life. His father's philosophy of life was to take advantage of others before they could take advantage of you. I remember stopping by his home one day with my son when we were home visiting my parents. I found a man who was lost, alone, and beaten down. He was so shocked by our visit that he began to weep as he walked out his front door.

I have often wondered what might have happened if his father had blessed his going to college on the scholarship he had been offered, instead of crushing his dream. Could that blessing have opened his life to new horizons? Might the different environment and new challenges have touched his life in such a way that his father's emotional dysfunction would not have consumed him? Would his life have had a different outcome if he had been encouraged to pursue his passion and his dream?

I am thankful to report that, some years after our visit, he met a very special woman. She was a person of faith who looked at him through different eyes and with a different heart. He soon found something in her that he had not experienced before, unconditional love. Where his life had been surrounded by criticism and the expectation of failure, he rebuilt his life and marriage upon his second wife's grace and encouragement. He is learning the beauty and blessing of being loved by someone who would sacrifice her own comfort so that he could realize his dream. I only wish it could have happened much earlier in his life.

In a classic sermon titled, "Message from an Empty Tomb," Dr. James Kennedy shares:

> For many centuries the men and women in Europe looked out upon the western sea, what we call the Atlantic Ocean, and they saw the sun coruscating upon the glittering surface of the waters, and they wondered. They wondered if there was anything beyond. Scholars said that you could sail off the edge of the world – there was nothing out there at all. In fact, inscribed on the escutcheons of the coat of arms of the nation of Spain was its national motto, *Ne Plus Ultra*, meaning, "There is nothing beyond."

> One day, Columbus went westering on the shiny waters. He sailed off into the sunset as people waited expectantly, and finally after a long time the sails reappeared and the crowds were exultant. They shouted with joy, and Columbus announced that there was a land beyond the sea that was rich beyond their dreams. It was a glorious paradise. The king of Spain changed the motto of that land until it reads as it does today, *Plus Ultra*, meaning, "'There is more beyond'" (Kennedy 1999, 66).

I had the opportunity to see the "more" in the life of a boy not more than eight years old. I was a part of a work mission trip to Honduras for the purpose of building homes. At the end of the week, everyone who had participated, both Hondurans and the North Americans, went to a restaurant to celebrate what had been accomplished. The meal was a highlight of the trip.

That day, outside the restaurant, we were met by many street children who beg in order to survive. One little fellow was shrewder than the others. The moment he saw us get out of the truck and walk toward the restaurant, he wrapped his arm around the waist of one of our men so that he looked like part of the work crew. He walked right past the security guard who kept the other children out.

I watched in amazement at how easily he navigated the situation. With laughter, he sat down at our table and we ordered him lunch. When our lunches came, the little boy covered his entire plate with a napkin. He then said something that none of us from the U.S. understood, but one of the Hondurans translated. "He wants you to know he will be gone for a few minutes but will be right back." He asked that we not let anyone take his lunch.

In a short while, we saw the door open and the little boy returned with his brother, about the age of four. It was evident that he would not take a bite until his little brother could eat also. He would not partake of his blessing without sharing it with another.

That moment was the humbling conclusion of our trip. We thought we had sacrificed in coming to Honduras to build houses for a week, but our sacrifice paled in comparison to this young boy's sacrifice for his brother.

THERE IS MORE BEYOND THE CONTINUAL GATHERING OF THINGS, OF HAVING OUR OWN WAY, AND OF HOARDING.

There is a world of blessing that only sacrificial love will open for us. There is a sense of fulfilment that only seeking the good of another will bring to our own hearts. There is more beyond the continual gathering of things, of having our own way, and of hoarding. There is a deeper understanding of meaning and purpose that pouring our lives into another will make possible.

In truth, dying to the old self leads to life in a new way. In Galatians 2:19–20, Paul writes, "I have been crucified with Christ. I myself no longer live, but Christ lives in me." Paul is not saying that a Christian must experience literal physical death on the cross, but he understood that we must compare our way of life to the selfless love of Jesus, then allow God's Spirit to remake us like him. Our current way of life must fall to the ground in order to let the new be born.

Remember what Jesus said in Matthew 10:39: "Whoever finds his life will lose it, and whoever loses his life for my sake will find it." *I have to give you up* is a life principle that we must follow if we want our loved ones to make a difference. My dad graciously released me and blessed my journey. In the thirty-eight years of ministry that have followed, God has graciously blessed Dad's giving. At its core, that is what a life of giving up is all about, releasing and blessing. It only happens when we love something or someone enough to give it up.

Discussion questions

1. What is the most difficult thing in life that you have had to give up?
2. What is the most difficult thing that you have not given up and are clinging to? Why?
3. What greater good is suffering as a consequence of your clinging?
4. Are you willing to ask some honest friends or advisors to share their observations about your willingness to surrender?
5. Will you pray for God to give you the strength to let go of what you love?
6. Will you then surrender what you love for the greater good?

10 CHAPTER

Different is a Good Thing

The Power of Diversity

MY DAD AND I WERE SIPPING SWEET TEA ONE AFTERNOON AS WE SAT IN THE rocking chairs that lined my parents' front porch. Some Southern traditions are just too wonderful to neglect. The pleasure of sharing a lazy afternoon on the front porch with my dad was one of those traditions, and we made it an art. Long pauses between pieces of conversation would be the norm; when nothing would be heard except the deep sighs of contentment and preparation for the next bit of self-proclaimed wisdom that would be shared. The Mississippi humidity was broken only by the faint breeze caused by the porch's overhead fans. Occasionally, we would drift back inside to refill our tea glasses or complete an afternoon nap. I miss those moments that shaped so many of my Saturdays and Sundays growing up.

On one particular occasion, we were reentering the house as I described a family that was rather eclectic and, you might say, "different." When I finished, Dad turned toward me and said, "Rolland, different is a good thing. In fact, different people make the world a better place. Imagine how boring the world would be if everyone was like you and me. Besides, there are only a couple of us perfect ones left…and I'm kinda worried about you!"

That simple conversation typified my father's willingness to rub elbows with all kinds of people. Rich or poor, red, black, yellow, brown or white, powerful or powerless, my dad treated all people with fairness and deference. He seemed to relish the opportunities to mingle with those different from him. A mentor and friend of mine, the late Dr. James Earl Massey, once told me, "Every person you meet has something to offer you. It is up to you to be wise enough to accept it." During my lifetime, I witnessed my father practicing that principle time and time again.

Being raised in Mississippi in the sixties when the civil rights movement was at its height, I had been exposed to many racial myths and prejudices. In fact, I had seen examples of prejudice at its worst and other memorable examples of overcoming prejudice. Two recent movies offer insight into my world during those days. *The Help* could have been a reality television series shot at my childhood home. We had a black maid named Minnie and, before her, a wonderful woman named Esther. They were both dear to our family and very instrumental in my life.

However, I now realize there were many hurtful moments in Esther and Minnie's lives, caused by our own covert prejudice. As I sat through the movie, I wept as I recognized the painful realities those two wonderful women had endured. When our boys were young, Ellen and I made certain that our sons got to know both Esther and Minnie. I wanted them to meet two incredible women who had influenced my life greatly. Esther and Minnie have both since died.

The movie *Mississippi Burning* also reflected some of the historical dynamics of my childhood years. The movie depicted the story of three civil rights workers who lost their lives doing voter registration in Neshoba County, Mississippi. They were consequently buried in an earthen pond dam by the Ku Klux Klan as retribution for their actions. That pond dam is located about thirty minutes from my childhood home.

So many memories come to mind as I reflect on growing up during those years of racial strife. I remember attending a high school football game at eight years of age. During the game, my friends and

I would gather past the end zone to play football, dreaming of the Friday nights we would actually be the players running out onto the high school field. One night during halftime, the KKK unexpectedly showed up and proceeded to burn a cross at the field. I remember being so frightened that I ran to my mom and dad in the stands. It was the first time I remember seeing the Klan in public.

A short time later, the KKK burned down Esther's church. In response to this horrible action, my grandfather bought an old gymnasium so that the materials could be used to rebuild Esther's church. The Ku Klux Klan then burned a cross in my grandfather's yard. Because he lived next door to our home, my parents would not allow me or my siblings to play in our front yard for several months. They feared that the Klan would drive by and shoot through our front windows. As a young boy, I was aware of the tension surrounding me, but did not really comprehend how combustible the situation was.

At age twelve, the federal government ordered the desegregation of our schools. On my first day of middle school, law enforcement officers were present on our school campus in case any problems occurred. (And I thought girls were going to be my biggest challenge in middle school!)

Throughout my junior high and high school days, athletics was a bridge-builder for me regarding race relations. One of my best friends in high school was a young black student, who is still the greatest athlete I have ever had the privilege of playing with. He was a person I admired deeply. Billie (not his real name) had no transportation; therefore, I would pick him up many afternoons for football and basketball practice. One evening after practice, I saw a fearful expression on his face when I invited him into my home to eat dinner with us. His response was, "Man, what are your momma and daddy goin' to say to you bringin' a nigger in the house?"

I said, "Billie, they won't think anything. They are not like that."

After a few moments inside, I shared that Billie and I were going into town to get something to eat. My father walked us to the car and warned us to be careful. He understood that there could be repercussions for friends of different races dining together in public at that time.

Even at an early age, I was confronted with the dissonance between the injustices I witnessed and the gospel I heard on Sundays. In the late 60's, I watched the video of Martin Luther King, Jr's speech, "I Have a Dream." I vividly remember being moved as he spoke for the equality of all people. However, Dr. King was not revered by everyone in our town; in fact, he was seen as a troublemaker. I often heard townsfolk express the opinion that he should leave well enough alone and not "mess with other folk's business." Yet my heart was torn between the prejudice I witnessed and the gospel I saw lived out by my parents.

Specifically, I remember an older black gentleman who always carried himself with grace and dignity. He worked in one of the local school systems, he held a terminal doctorate and was always dressed impeccably in a suit and tie. Each time my dad saw Dr. Jones (not his real name), he would take me over and reintroduce me to him. He always treated this gentleman with respect and deference. Dad expected me to shake his hand, refer to him as Dr. Jones, and respond to every question with, "Yes, Sir" or "No, Sir."

You might think this is nothing unusual, but when I was growing up in the South, older black people were expected to call a younger white person Miss or Mister. My dad would have none of that! By reintroducing me to Dr. Jones, I am certain my father intended to instill in me respect, no matter what color a person I might meet. I also believe he intended to show his own respect for this dignified gentleman.

I say this because there is a caveat to this story. My father said that when Dr. Jones was a young boy, a group of men pretended to hang him until he urinated in his pants. I believe my dad was ashamed that such a humiliating incident ever happened to such a good and kind person. My father's intentional elevation of Dr. Jones was an attempt to apologize for the hurt that prejudice and bias had caused in his life.

After graduating high school and a semester at a local community college, I choose to attend Anderson University, a small Christian university located in the Midwest. In this place, my own prejudices and biases were challenged by the faculty and a diverse student population. Soon people of different backgrounds became my dear friends. At every turn, they refuted the false truths and biases I had been surrounded with in the South as a child and teenager.

Because of these experiences, I underwent a change of attitude regarding my previous prejudices and biases, which I did not even realize I had. For that reason, my doctoral dissertation was written on the diversity experiences of undergraduate students at a private Christian university. I wanted to see if their experiences had the same life-changing impact they did on me. My research revealed that they did.

In the course of that research, I heard two words repeatedly: *prejudice* and *bias*. The words are defined as a strong inclination of the mind or a preconceived opinion or notion about something or someone. They entail making a judgment or assumption about someone or something before having enough knowledge to be able to do so with accuracy or clarity. As one looks more deeply into prejudice and bias, certain truths begin to emerge.

Truth # 1: All of us have prejudices and biases.

Every person some feelings or conceptions born out of prejudice or bias. Each of us has experiences and stories that influence how we think and act toward certain people or groups. None of us is without blemish in this area of our lives, because all of us have different perceptions of people that shape our thinking. If I were to call out different professions, your mind would automatically go to positive or negative perceptions you have of certain individuals within that profession. Those perceptions would be based upon past experiences you have had with other individuals within those professional frameworks. All of us have biases and prejudices because all of us have histories that influence how we think about others.

Truth # 2: Prejudice and bias cover multiple arenas of a person's life.

Race is only one aspect of prejudice. Prejudice can be linked to politics, lifestyles, personalities, socio-economic factors, education, gender, religion, and much more. They span a broad spectrum of our lives. Many times, we think our prejudice only affects our understanding of race, religion, or politics. The truth is, our lives are littered with multiple prejudices and biases because we are multifaceted people with thoughts and passions on a variety of topics. What is amazing is how we treat our prejudices as truth, simply because we have never been exposed to another truth that dispels or speaks to our biases.

Truth # 3: Prejudice and bias can be great hindrances to the flow of God's love and grace in our lives.

It is important to understand the potential for hurt and destruction that bias and prejudice can have in our lives. Prejudice can ultimately lead to anger and hate, which are often hidden inside us. We may not speak openly about it, but it is there. Over time, this anger takes root, causing a deep-seated bitterness and disdain that become embedded in our hearts. Bitterness and disdain impede the flow of God's love and grace within our lives, both to ourselves and others. Therefore, all of this hurt and destruction are by-products of the hate and anger within us.

In Ephesians 4:31–32, the apostle Paul speaks specifically of the harmful traits that prejudice and bias can create. He writes, "Get rid of all bitterness, rage, anger, harsh words, and slander, as well as all types of evil behavior. Instead, be kind to each other, tenderhearted, forgiving one another, just as God through Christ has forgiven you."

Notice the imperative phrase Paul uses: "Get rid of." Paul directs us to deal with the destructive issues that prejudice and bias can create inside us. It might be helpful to underline that phrase, because it brings to us a responsibility to deal with these issues in a manner that eradicates them from our lives and replaces them with traits that more clearly reflect this Jesus we profess.

I would like to say this is a simple process, but it is not. The adage, "Old habits die hard," is true. When a person has habitually been taught to think and act in a certain way, another way is difficult to take hold of. Prejudices and biases become innate. Jesus said in Luke 6:45, "A good person produces good things from the treasury of a good heart, and an evil person produces evil things from the treasury of an evil heart. What you say flows from what is in your heart" (NLT). These words better explain the truth that how a person thinks influences how that person acts and speaks. Changing what has habitually been stored and nurtured in one's heart is not easily done, but it can happen.

The story of Cornelius and Peter in Acts 10 clearly demonstrates this fact. This chapter recalls the moment when the New Testament church became aware that God desired to redeem not only people of Jewish origin but also those of a Gentile origin. In chapter 10, we find two men whose cultural biases and prejudices had taught them to disdain one another. Rest assured that Cornelius, a Roman centurion, and Peter, a Jewish leader in the Christian church, had not been taught to value or respect the other. The opposite was almost certainly true. Yet God chose to use them—a Jew and a Roman—to show how prejudice and bias could be overcome to better enable His love and grace to spread.

How did it happen? How did God take men from polar opposite views and enable them to overcome their biases in a way that allowed his grace and love to flourish? God confronted their bias and prejudice with the experiences they were about to engage in, and he did this through some incredible and intentional methods.

First, God moved supernaturally in both men's lives. This is usually the case. God most often begins with the human heart before transforming any other aspect of a person's life. It was so in the life of Moses, Nehemiah, and Paul, and here we see that the same thing happened in the life of Peter and a Roman centurion. In this story, Cornelius was approached by an angel and told to invite a Jewish evangelist to his home, while Peter was given a dream in which a voice told him that he could now eat foods that heretofore Jews were forbidden to eat. In each case, God challenged their prior thinking.

Often, before God can construct the new, the old has to be deconstructed and challenged. We also see that God works in supernatural ways to fulfill His greater plan for our good. While we think in immediate terms, God is always thinking strategically. While our view is narrowly focused like a tunnel, God's view is always panoramic. His ways are certainly not our ways and sometimes his divine methods transcend our normal methods of communication and action.

Second, God expected both men to humble themselves through obedient actions. God asked Cornelius to invite Peter, a Jewish believer, to come into his home and teach him. Cornelius certainly understood he held the position of power. At his beck and call, he could summon the power and strength of the Roman army. Yet Cornelius humbly allowed someone normally seen as an adversary to teach him and his household. It is important to note that Cornelius's heart was already being influenced by the touch and presence of God. However, some people in power find it isn't easy to practice humility.

God told Peter to enter Cornelius's home, he did—and he was embarrassed by the reception he received. Cornelius and his entire household bowed before Peter as he walked in the house. Peter quickly stated he was "only a man," perhaps remembering his past failures and being very cognizant of his current flaws and imperfections. Most people who have been broken in some way carry emotional scars that remind them they are really not "all that." Such humility is a key to overcoming bias and prejudice, because it is difficult to have a conversation when one person believes she/he is superior to the other.

Third, Peter swallowed his pride and talked openly about how God was changing his past perceptions. He said, "You yourselves know that it is unlawful for a Jew to associate with or to visit a Gentile; but God has shown me that I should not call anyone profane or unclean. So when I was sent for, I came without objection" (Acts 10:28–29).

FOR RESTORATION AND RECONCILIATION TO TAKE PLACE, SOMEONE MUST BE WILLING TO DO THE RIGHT THING.

For restoration and reconciliation to take place, someone must be willing to do the right thing instead of trying to be perceived as right. Sometimes pride and arrogance must be swallowed and mistakes acknowledged before collective barriers can be overcome. When individuals are willing to talk through issues openly and honestly, instead of simply holding on to past injuries, common ground can be found. Peter opened the door for reconciliation when he personally acknowledged that his prior perceptions of Gentiles were no longer valid because of what God was doing in his life.

Finally, God led both men to listen to one another. I have always believed that good things can happen when people are willing to talk and listen. In most cases, people are willing to talk; but sadly, very little listening often takes place. When all parties practice active listening, very positive results can occur. Listening allows multiple perspectives to be heard, and opens the opportunity to discuss and negotiate controversial issues. Listening creates an openness to have one's views challenged and to challenge another's views in a more informed manner. These conversations cause us to wrestle through what we believe and why we believe it.

In today's world, it is crucial for believers to have a solid understanding of their faith and not be embarrassed or uncomfortable in discussing those beliefs. Listening also establishes a greater tolerance and respect of others with differing beliefs (Engberg 2007, 285). When people are heard, they feel valued and believe that what they have to say matters.

While completing my doctorate, I encountered many diverse people in my classes. Two people brought diversity into my life in especially significant ways. One of them, Brian (not his real name), was a truly unique guy. His hair was long with a scraggly beard and he dressed as if he didn't know the sixties had passed. I didn't know Brian very well and I had my own preconceived notions of who he was.

Likewise, Brian wanted very little to do with me and he ignored or avoided me at all costs. I wasn't certain if he was uncomfortable with me as a pastor or if some of my comments during class had ostracized him. I took that as a challenge and was determined to get to know this guy. One night, during our class break, we were headed to the vending machines when I said, "Hi, Brian."

He turned and responded angrily, "You know what's wrong with you Christians? You do a lot of telling, but you don't do much listening."

"You know, you are probably right," I replied.

With that short conversation, he turned and walked off. Yet a relationship began that night and I worked very hard to continue it by listening well. We were as different as night and day, especially our belief systems. However, after listening to his story, I came to understand he was a good man who deeply cared for others. He was particularly committed to caring for the disenfranchised and those seen as outcasts by mainstream society. He challenged me constantly and would not allow my pat Christian comments to go without deeper explanations. In the long run, he made me a better person and strengthened my faith. After several classes and conversations, I respected him deeply and gladly called him my friend. I believe he felt the same way about me.

A second person who challenged my biases was Bea (also not her real name). Bea was bright, articulate, and a person who knew how to ask the right questions to get at the root of a problem. I watched with admiration how she could navigate difficult discussions with deliberate, intentional responses that very clearly staked her position without degrading or minimizing the other person involved. Several times, we had discussions over topics that would normally cause heated debates. Bea is a lesbian and I am a pastor who fully supports traditional marriage between a man and a woman. You can imagine the potential for conflict in this.

The most beneficial part of our discussions was that they didn't always focus on our differences but rather where we had come from and what made us who we were. In time, we began to know each other's stories and bits and pieces of our families. We both saw how hard the other worked to fulfill the dream that brought us back to school in our fifties, despite the obstacles that involved.

One day, I found out that Bea's mother had passed. I dropped by the funeral home for the viewing and sat with Bea's partner while Bea greeted those who came. After a while, she made her way over and said, "I can't believe you came here today."

"Why not?" I said. "You are my friend and you would do the same for me."

She replied, "You will never know what this means to me." I asked if I could pray for her and her partner before I left.

Later that year, I came to the day to defend my dissertation. It was a rigorous ordeal that lasted several hours. My wife and sons sat outside the room to encourage and pray for me during the arduous process, all the while hoping we would celebrate a positive outcome.

The defense went very well. Exhaustedly, I opened the door of the room to hug my family. Ellen then turned and said, "We are not the only ones who came support you." She pointed to her left. There sat my friend, Bea. I said, "I can't believe you came here."

She said, "Why not? You are my friend and you did the same for me." All of us hugged, smiled, and cried. It was a great moment to share with family and my friend.

Bea and I differ greatly in our perception of marriage, sexual relationships, and our belief as to how our faith undergirds that. But we base our friendship on mutual respect and kindness. Treating each other as friends did not change the fact that we had great differences and spoke forthrightly to each other about those differences. But our relationship was based on the belief that all people deserve respect and our actions represented that belief.

We must understand that prejudices and biases can greatly hinder the flow of God's love and grace in our lives, especially in our dealings with those who are different than us. When God begins to connect you with those you have prejudged and are uncomfortable with, take some initial steps toward reconciliation. First, humble yourself. Second, listen to the other person's story and see if that does not alter the way you hear them. Quit trying to prove you are right and simply respect the other person long enough to listen. If you do, you might discover what I did: The person who was so different, the person you had written off, has the potential to become a friend.

On this incredible journey of life, all of us carry prejudices and biases. But remember my dad's advice, "Rolland, differences are good things. Different people make the world a much better place. If everyone was like you and me, this world would be a boring place. Besides, there are only a couple of us perfect ones left, and I'm kinda worried about you!"

Discussion Questions:

1. In what areas of your life are prejudice and bias evident?
2. Has bitterness taken root in your heart or relationships because of it?
3. What steps do you need to take to get rid of that bitterness?
4. What steps toward restoration do you need to take? (humility, obedience, admitting wrong, listening, etc.)

11 CHAPTER

The Difference in Marriage

The Power of Giving One's All

IT WAS THE NIGHT BEFORE MY WEDDING. THE REHEARSAL AND REHEARSAL dinner had gone well. Even with all the people in town for the ceremony, my dad and I were able to steal a few moments alone together. Without any fanfare, which was always his style, he simply said to me, "Before tomorrow comes, I want to share with you what I consider to be the secret of marriage. Many people say that marriage is a fifty-fifty proposition. It isn't. The real difference in a marriage happens when both parties are willing to give 100 percent. If you will do that, Rolland—if you will always give Ellen 100 percent—then your marriage will be more than you ever imagined."

There I had it. In one small, concise statement, my dad had shared with me the principle that would not only make my marriage great but set it apart from most others. Dad had spoken from experience, as he and mom went on to share an incredible marriage for over sixty-seven years. Over the last 36 years, Ellen and I have tried to live out that principle in every facet of our marriage. We will both tell you that principle has made the difference in our marriage. Does it make marriage perfect and without struggles? No. But it does give couples a commitment to strive for complete mutuality. That is key: Always be centered on the commitment to give 100 percent, even when things aren't perfect.

Over our 36 married years, we have been in Christian ministry in one form or another. During this time, we have seen more marriages fall apart than we ever cared to. Many, many of these marriages had all the right tools to be successful; they just didn't have the right commitment to keep them on the right track. In almost all of these troubled marriages, about 90 percent of the time, the root causes of the struggles were selfishness and self-centeredness. Somewhere along the line, at least one of the spouses thought that the relationship was all about them. They had forgotten, or no one had explained, that true marriage is about both mates' giving 100 percent.

I do not want to make this sound too simplistic or easy, so allow me to explain the concept further. The principle of giving 100 percent means that my responsibility in marriage is to bless my wife. Plain and simple, the one dominant purpose in my relationship to Ellen is to bless her. In doing so, my greatest desire is to enable her to reach "her most blessable place" in life.

What do I mean by "her most blessable place"? Every person has needs, dreams, and desires. If that person is living in a place where those needs, dreams, and desires are being met or moved towards, then that is a blessable place. My role as Ellen's husband is to be aware and attentive to those needs, dreams, and desires, to understand them and then do everything in my power to help her fulfill each of those in the greatest way possible. When marriage is lived out at its best, each of us strives to do this for the other. That is called giving 100 percent and living to bless another human being.

However, most people coming into a marriage have preconceived notions about what they deserve or expect from their spouse. We all bring unspoken expectations into the marriage because of how we have seen relationships lived by those around us. In those relationships we have experienced both good and bad. In response to what we have seen modeled, all of us bring both positive and negative expectations into our marriages. The result of bringing negative expectations into marriage is that dysfunction gets passed down from one marriage to another, just like personality traits do. Therefore, every person enters marriage with expectations, some good and some dysfunctional.

There are two major problems with this scenario. First, most spouses are totally clueless about the expectations that are about to be laid on them, and people can't do what they don't know. Consequently, the marriage that began with unspoken expectations is now filled with the disappointment and frustration of unfulfilled expectations and the hurt of unmet needs. In the early days of most marriages, the husband and wife have not yet learned to talk and navigate through problems, therefore, the disappointment and frustrations become not only unspoken but also unresolved. The result is that the problems, disappointments, and frustrations only fester and grow into ongoing cycles of conflict and hurt.

When Ellen and I were first married, we had our own moments of unmet expectations. Believe it or not, our first major confrontation stemmed from my not taking out the garbage. Ellen and I grew up in homes with very different expectations for the husband and wife. Ellen grew up in the Midwest, where her father helped with most everything around the house from cleaning, cooking, and repairs to—you guessed it—taking out the trash. I was raised in a traditional Southern home where my dad did none of the household chores, as those tasks were taken care of by my mom. As I was growing up, I never saw my father clear the table, wash dishes, use a vacuum, or take out the trash.

After several months of being married, Ellen and I had just finished our evening meal. I got up from the table and walked past the extremely full trash can. She had seen enough. She turned to me in frustration and said, "Are you ever going to take out the trash? How can you walk past an overflowing trash can and not stop to take it out?" Trust me when I say the frustration was very evident in her voice.

I remember looking at her quizzically and saying, "I'm sorry. I didn't know I was supposed to take out the trash."

To Ellen, this thought was preposterous and offered in a cynical manner! She said, "My dad always took out the trash. I can't believe you don't know you're supposed to take it out!"

An unspoken expectation had just been communicated. Until that moment, I didn't know this had such importance. It became clear very quickly that I had failed at fulfilling it. However, that task has been handled promptly from that night forward! Now we both take out the trash as the importance of "whose job it is" has diminished over time. We laugh about this now, but the difference in how we were raised could have led to great conflict, had we not discussed how it would be handled.

Another critical issue for us has been how to resolve disagreements. Ellen is a processor and I am a let's-talk-about-it-now kind of person. I put Ellen in a difficult position when I expected her to line up with my Type A personality to talk through things before she has had time to process. While she still wants time to think about how to resolve a problem, she has learned it's not helpful to stew over issues until they became major problems. So we make it a priority to deal with issues while they are minor.

Every married couple deals with differences, dysfunction, and the frustration of unmet expectations. But candid, open-minded sharing goes a long way toward finding solutions.

Second, few people know that the most important thing we bring to a marriage is a servant's heart. If we allow personal expectations to overrule the desire to give and bless, our marriages become ledgers where the debits far exceed the credits and relationships end up in the red. That is not a place you want to be financially, and certainly not relationally or emotionally.

Servanthood is so important to a marriage because the only way love can be reciprocated in the right way is when love has been given selflessly. When we share our love with this intent, high expectations and stubborn selfishness die at the feet of selflessness and servanthood. Over time, selfless actions begin to set a foundational piece in place. The intent of this type of marriage is always to place the other in a blessable place. When this becomes the norm, selfless love is reciprocated and an incredible desire to love your spouse is cultivated in place of self-centered expectations.

Two scriptures speak specifically to the issues of servanthood and loving selflessly. I am going to take the liberty to change a few words to enable you to see how readily these verses speak to creating a blessable marriage. Jesus spoke of selfless love when he said, "No one can have greater love than to give his life for his *spouse*" (John 15:13 NLT).

The second passage is Philippians 2:2–7, where Paul writes regarding key components in becoming a servant, "Make my joy complete by being like-minded, having the same love, being one in spirit and of one mind. Do nothing out of selfish ambition or vain conceit. Rather, in humility value your *spouse* above your*self,* not looking to your own interests but each of you to the interests of the *other.* In your relationship with one another, have the same mindset as Christ Jesus: Who, being in very nature God, did not consider equality with God something to be used to his own advantage; rather, he made himself nothing by taking the very nature of a servant."

Over time, when one loves and serves like this, a marriage is filled with intentional blessings. "I live to bless you" would be the motto of this type of marriage. The hurts of unmet needs are slowly but intentionally replaced by the healing words and actions of affirmation, worth, and blessing.

Allow me to give you a word picture of what I am describing. On a vacation our family took out West, we were able to visit Mount St. Helens soon after it had erupted. The eruption had not only blown away a portion of the mountain, but its overflow and the power of the blast had destroyed hundreds of thousands of acres. Land that had once had a lush covering of fertile earth was stripped bare. The devastation was almost incomprehensible. This is similar to what many married couples experience when they try to conceal years of selfishness and self-centeredness. Their unmet expectations build until an explosion takes place. The aftermath is as devastating relationally as Mt. St. Helens was physically. Barrenness, emptiness, and lifelessness are the result.

In fact, there are many similar correlations. The landscape of a relationship can be stripped bare over time by selfishness. All the soil needed to produce a fruitful marriage is swept away by self-centered decisions. Eruptions of frustration only accelerate the erosion that has begun. Couples find themselves overwhelmed by the damage done by years of hurt and anger caused by unmet and unspoken expectations. *Barrenness* and *devastation* are not words normally used in reference to marriage, but in truth, they most accurately describe many hurting and damaged marriages.

However, nature has the capacity to accomplish an amazing feat at the site of a volcanic eruption. Slowly, the soil is replenished and new growth begins. It is not exactly the same growth as was present previously, because the soil has a different composition. Likewise, new growth in a replenishing marriage is not the same as newlyweds experience. Given the right soil, however—let's call it a blessable soil— grace, forgiveness, and wisdom can grow even in the most damaged marriages.

In their works, Seamands (1981) and Scazzero (2010) share critical steps toward healing where barrenness and devastation have been the prevalent landscape.

Step One: Face your problem squarely as a couple.

Many marriages miss deep inner healing because they lack the courage to face their fears and problems together. They have learned to ignore, cover up, and avoid discussing their dysfunction. But the Bible informs us that will not bring healing. James 5:16 states, "Confess your sins to one another, and pray for one another, that you may be healed" (NLT).

For healing to take place, honesty must replace lying, deception, and avoidance. If it doesn't, then healing has no soil in which to take root upon. The landscape is barren. The real issues must be brought up, discussed, worked through, and then put to rest. Remember, if you don't name it, you can't conquer it. It's like cleaning out a basement of clutter that has just sat undisturbed over the years. Unless you are willing to pick it up physically and carry it out of the house, the clutter will always remain.

In the same way, dysfunctional marriages are held hostage by repetitive dysfunctional issues. Look back over your marriage and see if the same trigger points set off continual angst in your relationship. I have yet to see any marriage find healing and wholeness without both spouses working diligently toward it. You cannot restore what you do not deeply want and fervently commit yourself to. You can always find a reason or excuse not to be reconciled, but you will never find healing until you do.

Second Step: Own your responsibility in the matter.

Most people in struggling marriages repeat the same lines:

**I was sinned against. She doesn't listen. He doesn't care.
I am the victim. I was wronged.
You don't know what I've been through and lived with.**

All the above could be true for almost anyone in a marriage over time, but what about you? What about the fact you have learned to hate and resent your spouse or escape into your own unreal world (Seamands, 1981, 24)? My father always told me, "There are two sides to every story." There is always blame enough to go around. The Bible makes clear that grievances involve two people. Colossians 3:13 says, "Bear with each other and forgive whatever grievances you may have against one another. Forgive as the Lord forgave you." In Mark 11:25, Jesus teaches, "And when you stand praying, if you hold anything against anyone, forgive him, so that your Father in heaven may forgive you your sins."

People with addictions must face this issue before they can move toward restoration. In Alcoholics Anonymous and Celebrate Recovery, before any person addresses the group, he/she must confess the dysfunction that holds her/him captive. Ask any person who has found help in dealing with personal hurts, habits, and hang-ups. That person will tell you they had to take personal ownership in the matter.

WE WILL NEVER RECEIVE HEALING FOR OUR DAMAGED
EMOTIONS UNTIL WE STOP BLAMING EVERYONE ELSE.

The truth is, we are all responsible for our actions. We will never receive healing for our damaged emotions until we stop blaming everyone else and accept our responsibility in the matter. If it takes two people to build a great marriage, it certainly takes two people to heal a damaged one.

Step Three: Be willing to go below the surface of the iceberg.

Emotionally healthy people are willing to take a deep hard look inside themselves and ask, "What is going on inside me that needs to change?" Trust me, this involves going beneath the surface of the iceberg that is called your home.

Scazzero (2010) writes that only about 10 percent of an iceberg is visible above the surface of the water. That is analogous to the part of our lives of which we are consciously aware (below the surface) and what other people are aware of (above the surface). What caused the Titanic to sink was not the small portion of the iceberg above the surface, but colliding with the 90 percent portion of the iceberg that was unseen. That is what also causes most shipwrecked marriages. We live inconsistent lives because we are unaware or unwilling to address the divisive forces that are below the surface (Scazzero, 71).

I admit it can be frightening to trust God's love and grace in order to look deeply inside oneself and admit we have struggles in our family or marriage. Yet one's heart is the wellspring and provider of life inside us (Prov. 4:23).

Those who have undergone open-heart surgery have discovered it is not the visible symptoms that caused the greatest danger to their health and well-being; it was the hidden blockage in the inner workings of the heart. If a heart patient fails to deal with those deeper issues, they will never experience healing. Those with untreated heart blockages face certain death or at least a life with great limitations. Married couples who are unwilling to address their own deeper issues also live with the same potential outcomes—the prospect of debilitation and death.

More than ten million readers have enjoyed Robert Boyd Munger's spiritually challenging meditation, *My Heart—Christ's Home*. Munger was a Presbyterian minister who wrote this timeless work in 1951. It tells the story of what it would be like to have Jesus come to the home of our hearts. Munger describes Christ's desires for us as He makes His way room by room through the human heart. In the living room, we prepare to meet Christ daily. In the dining room, we examine together what appetites should and should not control us. The struggle comes as Jesus desires to explore our private closets, those places in our lives that only we see. Jesus is not satisfied until we give him the key to our closets so he can help us deal with what is hidden inside (Munger 1986, 3–6).

So it is in a marriage that needs the healing power of Christ to restore it. No areas should be kept off-limits to the Lord's assessment. Even the deep dark places, far beneath the surface of the iceberg, must be brought forth and made available to the potential of healing. If not, the darker things below the surface will continue to shipwreck that marriage.

Step Four: Seek the help of a professional Christian counselor.

At times, all of us fear admitting our need for help. Christians may have a greater fear for the following reasons:

1. Admitting our need is admitting our spiritual weakness, and we see that as declaring that God is not able to get us through our struggles.
2. We fear that others will judge us or our faith as weak if we admit our need for help.
3. We have been told that with enough prayer and faith, we can do for ourselves what needs to be done.

Ironically, when our children are involved in sports or the arts, we readily find them coaches or teachers to help them develop their abilities and competencies. When they struggle in school, we find tutors to help them. Why then are we averse to seeking professional help when it comes to restoring our marriage or family? If we wanted to build a new addition on our home, most of us would bring in a professional carpenter to do the work. Yet when it comes to the relational or emotional rebuilding of our home or marriage, we think we will appear weak to ask for help and guidance.

The Bible speaks clearly regarding the humility needed to gain and ask for wisdom. Proverbs 4:7 says, "Wisdom is supreme; therefore, get wisdom. Though it cost all you have, get understanding," In Proverbs 13:10, we read, "Pride only breeds quarrels, but wisdom is found in those who take advice."

If your marriage is struggling and you've been wrestling about it for a long time, what personal action do you and your spouse need to take to change things? You can pray for it and wish for it, but at some point, you have to act differently to bring about positive change. One of those actions is to connect with a Christian counselor to help you navigate the white waters of life.

AT SOME POINT, YOU HAVE TO ACT DIFFERENTLY
TO BRING ABOUT POSITIVE CHANGE.

Have you ever been white-water rafting? The first time our family rafted was at the New River Gorge in West Virginia. I was impressed with the thorough preliminary instructions our guide required all participants to understand before we entered the rafts. After the instructions, the guide asked who wanted to ride in the front of the raft. Before I could take a breath, our oldest son Tyler, who was ten at the time, yelled, "My dad and I do!"

What was I going to do? I smiled sheepishly as the guide called us up front and gave us more specific instructions about where to place our feet, how to paddle into a wave, and how to keep our bottoms on the seat when going over a ledge. We learned all this in a span of about five minutes. To say I felt inadequately prepared was an understatement!

After the rafting trip was over, I was so thankful Tyler had volunteered us for the special up-front seating assignment. I will never forget the thrill on his face as we made our way down the river, crashing through waves and floating through currents so strong they could capsize or pull the raft under. Yet I was even more thankful that a guide made the journey with us. I couldn't imagine trying to make that trip without the experience and expertise of our guide, who helped us navigate the waters we plowed through at breakneck speeds.

In some ways, life in a struggling marriage is a lot like navigating the rapids of a river. If you are not familiar with handling the unforeseen currents and reading the signs of the river, you are much more susceptible to capsizing. Sometimes couples need experienced counselors to function as guides when navigating the white waters of their marriage. It is so important not to let pride stand in the way of taking hold of whatever help is needed to turn your marriage around. Remember the warning of Proverbs 16:18, "Pride goes before destruction, and haughtiness before a fall" (NLT).

Perhaps God would bring healing to your family and marriage through the giftedness of a Christian counselor. I have benefitted from seeing a personal counselor and I know many others who have benefitted from this type of godly wisdom and skill.

Healing can happen in a marriage when selflessness starts replacing the deep-rooted attitudes of selfishness and self-centeredness. Slowly and intentionally, a marriage's devastated soil can be replenished with blessable soil. When this happens, new growth begins to take place. As with the area surrounding Mount St. Helens, new growth begins only as a green patch or two at a time, but it is a beginning. And a beginning is good. Healing from any wound never happens overnight. Remember, growth makes way for newness, but the process does take time.

Our oldest son, Tyler, was born with spina bifida. This birth defect occurs when the spine and spinal cord don't form properly. There are different levels of severity. When Tyler was first born, the medical team that evaluated him said there was a good chance he would never walk. At the very least, he would have serious neurological problems, possibly mental problems or delays, and doctors detected what they thought was a severe heart murmur. Even though Tyler has endured nine surgeries (a small number compared to some with spina bifida), at one time he was a head golf pro. God blessed our son in miraculous ways, for which we are extremely grateful.

Ty's beginning was anything but normal or easy. He was hospitalized for the first seven weeks of his life and underwent two surgeries before he was six weeks old. During the duration of this initial hospital stay, a hospital social worker was intent on meeting with Ellen and me. To be honest, we avoided her at every turn because we were mentally, physically, and emotionally exhausted. We wanted to talk to as few people as possible, especially a stranger that we thought would want to chat about the fears we had regarding our son's health and the unknown future he now faced.

One day, Ellen and I were in the radiology area waiting for Tyler to have yet another CAT scan when the door burst open. The social worker came in and leaned on the door as she closed it behind her. In essence, she had us trapped! Immediately, she said, "I know I am the last person on the face of the earth you want to talk to right now. But we need to talk, because almost 90 percent of all marriages that have a child born with spina bifida end in divorce."

She now had our full attention. We listened closely as she explained to us the pressures that might be placed on our marriage over the next several years, depending on how Tyler progressed physically and the struggles he might incur. That evening, after Tyler's final night feeding, we walked across the hospital parking lot to my parents' motor home to sleep for a few hours, as we had done nightly for the past several weeks. Only this night, we stayed up even later, talking about what we had learned that afternoon. After some reflection, we made a commitment to one another that we have kept for over 36 years:

> **No matter what this life journey throws at us, no matter how much pressure we feel or how tired and weary we get, no matter what steps we have to take to give Tyler or any future children the best care we can, we will always walk toward each other and never, ever walk away from each other.**

Was this commitment a cure-all for the challenges that lay ahead? Absolutely not. Were there still tough times and difficult moments? Absolutely, yes. In all truth, during some of the most severe of Tyler's surgeries, we confided in friends that we literally felt life go out of us. Then there was the financial pressure. It took us eleven years to pay off the cost of our child's initial birth and hospital care. At times, our unknown burdens seemed greater than our physical and spiritual capacity to carry them. With the last surgery Tyler endured for a tethered spinal cord, the doctors feared his ability to walk would be grossly limited or lost completely. Thank God, the surgery went better than we ever hoped. In all these hard moments, we held to our commitment not to let go of each other. We would always walk toward one another and never away from each other.

Believe me when I say that marriages can flourish in the soil of blessing, affirmation, and worth, even marriages that have struggled previously or marriages that are in the midst of struggles now. I know this because I have witnessed marriages that have reproduced this type of soil in the midst of barrenness. It is never easy, and it is not without great effort and sacrifice.

I truly believe some marriages make it and others don't because of what my dad said: Both partners must be willing to give 100 percent. When barren soil is replaced with a soil rich of affirmation and shared worth, a married couple can truly start the process of redemption and restoration because their marriage becomes a blessable place.

Discussion questions

1. How would you describe the spiritual soil of your marriage, you family, or your workplace? Is it barren, toxic, untilled, fertile, or blessable?
2. What negative dynamics need to be replaced to create a blessable place in your marriage and family?
3. What expectations do you bring to your marriage?
4. Have you described those expectations to your spouse?
5. Describe to each other what actions make you feel loved, cherished, and valued.

12 CHAPTER

Perception is 90 Percent of Reality

The Power of Understanding What Others See

HAVE YOU EVER BEEN IN A SITUATION WHERE PEOPLE WERE NOT RESPONDING in the way you hoped or expected them to? If you have spent any time in leadership, the answer is yes. The more relevant question might be, have you ever been in a situation where people responded *exactly* the way you hoped or expected them to? At times, the task of interacting with other human beings can be perplexing and exhausting to say the least.

On one occasion, I was experiencing this with a group of persons in a dramatic and painful manner. I was discussing with my dad about how wrong their reactions were and how amazed I was that they felt the way they did. "If they would only look at the facts," I said, "they would see the truth for what it is."

My dad laughed and said, "Rolland, that is probably not going to happen because their vision of truth is not yours. They have a different perception of the situation and perception is 90 percent of reality." Over the following weeks and months, I pondered his words and concluded he was right. In real life and real time, all of our beliefs and thoughts are colored and influenced by our perceptions. We see it lived out over and over again in our everyday lives.

For instance, how I respond to you is determined in many ways by the perceptions I formed of you when we first met. As badly as I may not want to, that initial perception is about 90 percent of my reality regarding you. Add to the equation that each individual in each situation brings individual perceptions to each group and we better understand what complicates every situation a leader faces.

Now just imagine when those dynamics are multiplied by hundreds or thousands of individuals that make up large organizations and complex groups. Past experiences, personalities, emotional ties, insecurities, and sentimental values all enter the picture and the result is complex personal perceptions that dominate each person's reality.

Moses experienced this when he led the Israelites out of Egypt. They had not even reached a new a Zip Code when someone noticed Pharaoh in hot pursuit. The Israelites begin to clamor at Moses, "Have you brought us out here to die, because there was no good place to bury us in Egypt?" Certainly, Moses had to have been both perturbed and perplexed. Yet his initial actions and words seemed intended to alter the Israelites' preconceived perceptions of themselves.

Their time in Egypt had ingrained in them a self-perception as oppressed slaves. They saw Egypt as the dominant master and themselves as those who would always be dominated. They were reacting in the way they had always been taught: Submit to the greater authority. For Moses to help them change their minds and posture, he would need to change their self-perceptions. Therefore, in Exodus 14:13, he instructs them, "Don't be afraid. Just stand still and watch the LORD rescue you today. The Egyptians you see today will never be seen again. The LORD himself will fight for you. Just stay calm" (NLT).

Then God did the impossible. He divided the Red Sea down the middle and allowed them to cross over on dry ground. As the army of Pharaoh entered the water, Moses withdrew his staff and the walls of water collapsed on the Egyptians and drowned them all. In doing all of this, a new perception and reality were born in the hearts and minds of the Israelites. A new master and leader had come into their lives. He was Yahweh God. And a new reality of self-thought was being created. They were no longer slaves but God's chosen, loved, and valued children. Moses understood that if you really want to change others' outlook, then help change their personal perceptions. It also doesn't hurt to spend forty years in the desert transforming the culture.

Gifted leaders understand that every situation they encounter is colored by the perceptions of the people they lead. No situation is lived out in a vacuum. Therefore, a scientific strategy based on facts and figures will never fully address a problem because it does not encompass the emotional and relational dynamics that every situation is influenced by. A human being's life is much more complicated than that. One of the greatest errors any leader will ever make is underestimating this truth and how it will influence every situation, even when trying to bring what is personally perceived as positive change.

Here are some simple steps to follow in evaluating perception before making crucial decisions.

Listen to others' stories before determining the final story.

It sounds rather elementary, but the importance of listening to why people have differing perspectives is critical and the results can head off a multitude of problems. Most people are not hesitant to share their stories if only asked. The trick is listening long enough to fully grasp what they're saying. If a leader will do this, the critical values and perceptions underlying issues can be discerned. It is much easier to find the proper solution if you first define the values and perceptions in play. Perhaps the most important ability any leader will ever learn is the crucial art of listening.

The story is told of a phone call coming into a local congregation's office. The Administrative Assistant graciously answered the phone and a voice said, "Hello, is the head hog in?"

The Administrative Assistant replied indignantly, "Excuse me?"

The person on the other end of the line repeated, "I said, is the head hog there?"

To that, the Administrative Assistant responded, "Pardon me, Sir, but I am not sure who you are referring to. If you are referring to our Senior Pastor, I do not appreciate your speaking of him in that way."

The caller quickly responded, "Please, please excuse me. I meant no disrespect. My name is Gus Johnson and I am a pig farmer. You see, my wife and I just sold our pig farm for six million dollars and we want to give the church half of that."

There was a long pause on the other end and then the Administrative Assistant said, "Just a minute and I'll see if the Old Pig is here!"

Imagine what a mistake it would have been had the Administrative Assistant not listened to the farmer's complete story. Amazing how her response changed when she listened to enough of farmer's story to understand his playful intentions! Remember, it is always easier to define the proper solution if you first define the values and perceptions in play.

Listen to your critics as much as you do your fans.

In truth, this is one principle I wish I had cultivated better early in my leadership journey. I remember two specific occasions when perceptions different than my own were shared with me. The first was in a congregation I had been pastoring for about three years. The staff and I had presented a new ministry idea to the governing board and received their approval. Later that week, one of the board members came by my office and asked to speak with me. He was a man I deeply respected and shared a great relationship with. His initial comment was, "Rolland, you know I deeply value your leadership, but I don't think this is the best time for this new initiative. I just don't think the congregation is quite ready for this type of change. I hope you'll reconsider the timing of it."

He was right. We delayed the launch until later and it was received without reservation. His perception, formed over twenty years at that congregation, brought wisdom to my three-year perception. A few weeks later, I took him aside and thanked him for "saving my bacon."

His willingness to share his input had stopped me from making a painful mistake.

After I had been at a different congregation for several years and dealt with many difficult issues, I was visited one day by a gentleman who had been a part of some of those difficult moments. This was not unusual, since he had continually expressed both his approval and disapproval of my leadership over the years. That day, he suggested that we reverse some of the changes we had made years before. I knew that he had not embraced the changes in the beginning and felt he was simply trying to get things back to the way they were before. But when he rose to leave my office, he said, "Pastor, I just have a feeling there is some dissonance in the church and I want to do everything I can to head it off before it boils over." I thanked him for his time and he left.

Two years later, the church went through a difficult experience. The incident was not directly tied to his suggestion, but in hindsight I wish I had investigated his parting comment more fully. Perhaps I could have averted some of the fallout if I had.

As I reflect on how I responded to both situations, it occurs to me that my response had been influenced by my previous experiences with both men. One had been a constant friend and ally while the other had mostly been a critic. The lesson I learned is don't be too quick to dismiss the perceptions of your critics. In your efforts to better understand their differing perspective, you may come to realize they have a different perception for a good reason. In the long run, it might even save you unnecessary angst, emotional energy, and the pain of broken relationships. On the other hand, your efforts may better convince you that your perception is solid and you can move ahead with greater confidence. Either way, the outcome can be a positive and valuable one.

Don't base your perception on what you choose to make important.

It is so much easier to design a specific strategy to address a problem if you are aware of and working within the actual perceptions, thoughts, feelings, and dynamics involved in the situation. If the leader is not aware of these dynamics, he/she may compensate by addressing the issue to fit his/her predisposed predilections and miss the real problem all together. This is a matter of the leader choosing what to heed, based solely on personal likes and dislikes.

In such a situation, a leader should ask some critical questions:

1. Is my perception of reality based solely on my own perception?

To honestly answer this question, the leader will probably need to ask others to speak candidly into his/her life. It is important to choose people who are with and without bias, inside and outside the issue. It is important to hear from those inside the arena and folks who don't have a bone to pick or a "dog in the fight."

2. What steps must I take to gain a better and bigger perspective?

Every leader must be willing to do the homework necessary to gain a deeper understanding of the issue at hand. Surveys, town-hall meetings, small chat groups, one-on-one conversations with involved parties—these can all be utilized to gain a bigger and better perspective. After gathering the needed information, it is important to communicate and verify results before hitting the fast-forward button and acting. Yes, asking these questions takes time and effort, but they are always worth the cost. In fact, the cost may be far greater if the time is not taken.

Don't let your perception be overly influenced by your insecurities.

The principle that "self-perception is 90 percent of reality" is even more important for individuals who desire to better understand themselves to address the issue at hand. The truth is, we all have insecurities that influence our decisions. Your inner truth regarding yourself is based on how you perceive yourself. This inner truth is a compilation of how you have heard others describe you, the crowns or scars your past has awarded or afflicted upon you, and the messages your current reality communicates to you. In other words, don't let the past determine your present perception.

You see, our personal perceptions were not created in a day. Our lives are giant canvases that have been painted over the duration of our time spent on this earth. For some of us, these canvases have captured helpful and hopeful views. For others of us, they have created a hurtful, critical, and damaging perception of reality. In the middle is where we find the truth, as most of us are a mixture of both. To recognize and overcome the negative traits that have been established in us will not be easy and it will not happen without intentional effort. There are a couple of reasons this is true.

First, our past can diminish our expectations in the present. We are like a flea in a jar. We will only jump so high because hitting the ceiling on the first few tries has convinced us to jump only with minimal expectations. Most of us have events from the past that have limited our present in some fashion. We need to zero in on those events and then work to minimize the limitations. Please know, it is difficult to realize the full potential of the present if our past still dominates our thinking.

Second, our past can limit what we ask or believe in the present. Have you ever visited the Grand Canyon? It is an overwhelming sight. However, did you know there are people who visit the Grand Canyon but never see it? Their fear of heights will not allow them to make their way to the sides of the canyon to take in its vastness. Therefore, their limited view narrows their capacity to see the grandeur of the whole. For some of us, our past fears or experiences limit our view of God, therefore limiting what we believe and ask God for in the present.

In Matthew 28 and Acts 1, Jesus speaks to His disciples regarding the need to go and expand the Kingdom. "I have been given all authority in heaven and on earth. Therefore, go and make disciples of all the nations, baptizing them in the name of the Father and the Son and the Holy Spirit" (Matt. 28:18–19 NLT). "But you will receive power when the Holy Spirit comes upon you. And you will be my witnesses, telling people about me everywhere—in Jerusalem, throughout Judea, in Samaria, and to the ends of the earth" (Acts 1:8 NLT).

Both passages reflect what we call the Great Commission, but in some ways they could also be called the Great Reminder. In both passages, Jesus speaks of His authority and power resting on these very ordinary people. Jesus reminds them that, yes, there was a crucifixion in their past, but their future will be determined by the power and authority of the resurrection, not the limitations of the tomb. Sometimes we also need to be reawakened to the Great Reminder so we do not allow the hurtful parts of our past to limit or diminish our present. The same resurrection power and authority that lived in the disciples can also live in us.

Perhaps some of the greatest redemptive work that Jesus does in any human being's life is when He helps transform the perception we have of ourselves and of others. Many times, our greatest limitations are linked to how we perceive ourselves as limited or damaged. In the same way, many of our insecurities are linked to how we perceive others as better, hurtful, arrogant, or intimidating. The Good News brings with it the possibility of seeing ourselves as whole because Jesus has the capacity to make all things new. The "new thing" mentioned in Isaiah 43 can pertain to our lives! Notice this promise: "This means that anyone who belongs to Christ has become a new person. The old life is gone; a new life has begun!" (2 Cor. 5:17 NLT).

Over the past few years, I have taught a Bible study at a place called Man 4 Man Ministries, which helps previously incarcerated men find their way back into society. To be precise, Man 4 Man helps men reinvent their lives by introducing them to the Giver of life, Jesus. Bob Bloom, the founder and director of the ministry, is a dear friend and mentor of mine. After I finish teaching and sit down, Bob comes forward and asks the men what they took from the teaching. These are the moments when I sit in awe of how the gospel can change lives in such transformational ways.

One man started sharing about the day he found a young man breaking into his car. This man had a violent past and so, without hesitation, he jumped in his car and started chasing the young man who was getting away on a bicycle. During the short chase, he positioned his car in a way that cut the young man off and caused him to wreck. In a flash, he was out of his car and on top of the young man, straddling him. Without thinking, he raised his massive fist in the air, about to pound the young man's head into the pavement. In his previous life, he would have done this without any hesitation. But now he was a different man with a different perception of life, so he looked at the young man and then looked at his raised fist. He took a breath, changed his raised fist to a raised hand, and said to the young man, "You need to find Jesus."

A great moment in the journey of transformation is when we come to understand that wholeness is not determined by how others view us or have treated us. Our wholeness depends on the perception that we have been redeemed and made new. That perception allows us to stand in a different place with a different view, a view that is no longer dependent on the transactions of the past but on the redeemed present that only Jesus can make possible.

We must begin where the Israelites did as we work to create a new perception of ourselves. The voices that created our damaged perceptions must be replaced with a new language of the heart. Where there was hurt, we must begin to hear God speak healing to us. Where there was criticism, we must begin to hear God speak encouragement. And where there was ridicule and put-downs, we must begin to hear God speak value and affirmation to us as His child.

I have witnessed too many people whose destructive pasts have created for them a destructive present. But in the same way, I have witnessed those, like the gentleman noted above, whose lives have been transformed by receiving the unconditional love of God.

Let me share a story regarding one of the legends of the Christian faith. I would suspect you have probably never heard of Gladys Aylward. She was affectionately called the Mouse because of her slight stature and build.

In her younger years, Gladys was a domestic servant in London, earning pennies a week. After reading a magazine article about China, she had a lingering sense that God desired her to minister in this country. The problem was that no one else perceived she had the ability or strength to fulfill that calling. She was rejected by the China Inland Mission group; all other doors she tried to open were shut in her face.

Yet Gladys Aylward would not allow the perceptions of others to determine her perception of herself or the belief that God could use her. Finally, she cried out, "O God, I possess almost nothing. But here is my Bible, here is my money, and here am I! Use me!" With that, she began saving money to purchase a one-way ticket to China. Months and months went by until she could buy the ticket and board a train that made its way through Communist Russia. In the middle of the night, the train was halted by Communist soldiers and Gladys was cast off the train in the middle of a snowstorm with only her suitcase, which contained everything she owned.

Remarkably, the Mouse would not be dissuaded by the soldiers or the weather, so she made her way to the nearest town and found shelter. After several days, a young woman approached her and said, "You must leave immediately. You are in grave danger because the secret police plan to send you to a work camp. A man will come for you tonight and you must follow him and do exactly what he instructs you to do."

Hours later, a man appeared out of the shadows and led her through dark alleys until they reached an ocean dock. He said as he pointed to the water, "Over there you will find a Japanese freighter. Whatever you have to do to get on that ship, you must do it and leave Russia tonight." As providence would have it, the captain of the ship allowed her to board. Days later, Gladys arrived in Kobe, Japan, where she boarded a steamer to China.

In 1932, more than ten years after her initial sense of calling, she finally set foot on Chinese soil. Her ministry in that country lasted 38 years until her death in 1970 at the age of 68. Despite her diminutive size of only 5 feet tall and less than 100 pounds, despite her lack of schooling, and despite others' perceptions that she was not capable or qualified, Gladys Aylward influenced a country for her faith. At the end of her ministry, she was sought out by mission leaders and government officials alike. All because Gladys Aylward would not allow others' perceptions to overrule what she believed God's perception of her was.

Take a moment to meditate on the apostle Paul's words in Romans 12:2: "But let God transform you into a new person by changing the way you think" (NLT).

TRANSFORMATION HAPPENS ONLY WHEN THE
LEGALISM OF RELIGION IS REPLACED WITH
A PERSONAL RELATIONSHIP TO JESUS.

This happens only when your self-perception is changed from unlovely to lovely, from weak to strong, and from unworthy to worthy. It happens only when you replace the legalism of religion with a personal relationship that Jesus and His redemptive grace bring.

I know this is not always an easy path. Many times, it is a journey of two steps forward and one step back. It is hard to overcome the pain that your past may have caused you, but through the power of a redemptive Savior, it can be done. I have walked this path and am walking it today. But I must constantly remind myself that the gift of redemption brings with it the potential of a new day and fresh start. Galatians 5:1 makes this abundantly clear. "Christ has set us free to live a free life. So take your stand! Never again let anyone put a harness of slavery on you" (Gal. 5:1, The Message).

Stand up and do whatever is necessary to remove the perceptions that have hindered you. Change your perceptions about who you really are because, as Habey's words remind us, "Perception is 90 percent of reality." Today, you can take hold of a new reality!

Discussion questions

1. What self-perception has your past painted for you?
2. Are individuals in your life moving you toward a more positive self-perception?
3. If not, what steps need to take place to make this transition happen?
4. In dealing with difficult situations, do you work hard to understand other people's feelings or perceptions?
5. What knowledge or value might you gain by listening to others?

13

The Difference Between
Confronting and Destroying

The Power of Constructive Conflict

IT WAS ONE OF THOSE DAYS I DIDN'T WANT TO BE A LEADER. I HAD JUST BEEN told that one of my laypersons was guilty of a moral failure. Now it was up to me to confirm whether this accusation was true.

As always when handling a difficult situation, I called my dad before taking action. He was the rock that my siblings and I leaned on in any difficult situation. I described the situation and asked for his advice. After sharing with me his thoughts and assuring me that he would pray for me to have wisdom, he said one final thing: "Rolland, remember this. There is a difference between confronting someone and destroying someone. You can confront the issue without destroying that person's life. Let that be your goal. If you keep that in mind, you'll handle the situation the right way."

I thought about Dad's words long and hard before I met with the person the next day. I realized that I might help to destroy this person's life or give them an opportunity for repentance and restoration. Thankfully, they confessed their wrong and we were able to begin a process of healing. Their role as a lay leader, although different, was restored.

Dad had reminded me that for confrontation to be effective, it should be done forthrightly, but also with grace, redemption, and wholeness in mind. At the same time, the attitude of the person confronted will determine the outcome. Grace, mercy, and accountability must be appropriately received.

Sadly, I have known other situations in which the outcome was far different. The offender rejected an opportunity for repentance and redemption, so the outcome was altogether different. However, the important principle shared by my dad still holds: There is a great difference between confronting and destroying.

Jesus demonstrated this when a woman was caught in adultery and brought before him. Religious leaders wanted her emotional humiliation and physical death. They felt they had a right to pursue this with fervor. From a legalistic point of view, they did have that right.

On the other hand, Jesus approached the situation in an entirely different manner. With grace and mercy, he offered an opportunity for redemption. His intent was to confront, but not to destroy the person being confronted. Jesus' confrontation of the wrong was buffered by His desire to offer redemption to the one who had done the wrong. His closing comment to her reveals this. "Neither do I condemn you," Jesus declared. "Go now and leave your life of sin."

Now that I look back, that is exactly what my dad was saying to me. I needed to confront that layperson. That is often the responsibility of a leader. If you lead for any significant amount of time, you discover that confrontation is a part of your job. Wrongs must be confronted and people held accountable for their actions. It is not an easy part of leadership, but it definitely is a part of the responsibility. When those times come, how you confront someone will make all the difference.

Confrontation is not what I enjoy most in my ministry. In fact, it was a skill that I knew I didn't have early in my ministry. When confrontation took place, it deflated me emotionally and I often needed days to recover from the drain.

Over time, it became clear that if I desired to stay in leadership, I had to learn how to confront others constructively. I had to admit that my emotional wiring made this role difficult because the "people pleaser" in me hated the notion of any conflict, while the perfectionist in me felt I had failed if I needed to confront someone in my care. In spite of these barriers, I had to learn the skill of constructive conflict.

Sad to say, in all my academic and theological training, I had never been taught how to handle constructive conflict. (Notice I said *constructive* conflict because conflict has the potential to be either constructive or destructive. Along the way, I have learned some valuable lessons, most of them modeled for me by other ministry leaders. However, I must admit that some of my conflict skills were learned painfully as I stubbed my own toe and stepped on the toes of others in the process.) Here are ten steps toward constructive conflict that I have learned:

1. Determine if the issue is really worth personal confrontation. A personal mentor once said, "Remember, fewer people die from a side swipe than from a head-on collision." Sometimes the best decision in a conflict is to walk away and let time take its course. That decision depends on how we answer the following three questions.

Is this truly my issue or am I owning something that is not really mine? For those who have a high sense of justice, this is easier said than done. Such people see things in black and white with very little room for shades of gray. They are always ready to take up a cause and own it, even if it's not theirs to own. Over time, high-justice folks invest more emotional energy and damage more relationships than they need to.

Will the end result be worth the cost? Every decision has a cost, even the decision to do nothing. As leaders, we must assess if the outcome will be truly worth the cost to the organization, to others, and to us as individuals. If we conclude that it costs more than its worth, we shouldn't do it. We should let sleeping dogs lie.

Will the result make a lasting difference? A great way to answer this question is to hypothetically look six months down the road and ask yourself if the decision will truly bring lasting and positive change for the organization. If not, then it's probably not worth the energy it will take. Lay it down and move on to something that really matters.

2. Never make confrontation personal, make it about the issue. Anytime a confrontation becomes personal, then the issues may not be resolved. Personal injury hurts, offends, strikes out, and strikes back. Individuals involved in personal disputes have the tendency to become offensive and defensive at the same time. Many people don't play fair when things get too personal.

That is why you should take some preventive steps if you sense this is becoming a matter of personal differences. First, ask a non-biased party to be present when the issue is being discussed. This will allow a neutral voice to speak into the discussion and give accountability to the parties involved. If sarcasm or personal attacks begin creeping into the dialogue, the non-biased party can bring the conversation back to the issue at hand and move toward a constructive outcome.

Second, determine whether there really is an issue or simply a personal conflict. Perhaps you don't need to work through an issue of policy, finance, or any other managerial problem; perhaps you need to work through emotional conflicts within yourself. Sometimes our perceived disagreements with the policies of others have more to do with our personal needs and insecurities than the policy issue we blame for our needs and insecurities. If candid reflection reveals that's true in your case, then own it and find someone to help you work through your own stuff. Don't blame others for your personal shortcomings.

3. Allow any anger or frustration to subside before confronting. Proverbs 13:3 states, "He who guards his lips guards his life, but he who speaks rashly will come to ruin." Sad to say, the latter part of this verse is too many times the path chosen in confrontation. When this happens, we *react* to a situation instead of *responding* to it. Did you catch that? We react when we should have responded. We turn our frustration into an attack of someone else in an effort to "get it out of our system and deal with it." Proverbs 15:18 makes this perfectly clear: "A hot-tempered person starts fights; a cool-tempered person stops them" (NLT).

When anger drives our responses, we throw gas on the proverbial fire and abandon any effort to maintain a calm demeanor. Certainly, with any emotional issue it is wise to give it the "One Night's Good Sleep" rule. If you can't sleep because of your anger and frustration concerning the issue, then wait another night to process the emotions at hand. That additional night might give Ephesians 4:29 a better chance to become reality: "Do not let any unwholesome talk come out of your mouths, but only what is helpful for building others up according to their needs, that it may benefit those who listen."

4. Pray and ponder long enough to approach the situation with wisdom beyond yourself. I am a firm believer that prayerful pondering makes us much wiser than we normally would be. If we need to take anything else into these types of discussions, it would be the wisdom of someone wiser than ourselves. God's wisdom, for example. Take some time to get away and ask God who is wise enough to give you guidance and direction in this situation. The apostle James assures us this option. "If any of you lacks wisdom, he should ask God, who gives generously to all without finding fault, and it will be given to him" (James 1:5).

We are all limited in our understanding. Perhaps God envisions a greater work than the one we are contemplating. We will never capture this unless God divinely engages and intervenes in our thoughts and conversation to reveal his greater truth and plan at hand. This will certainly never happen if we have not previously made room at the table for God to join and lead the discussion.

In Psalm 86, David petitions God to reveal for His greater way and truth to be revealed, not to bring honor to the psalmist, but so that his actions may bring honor to God. "Teach me your ways, O Lord, that I may live according to your truth! Grant me purity of heart, so that I may honor you" (Psa. 86:11 NLT).

Believers truly do hope and pray to act according to God's greater way for His Kingdom's sake. This is not always easy or simple when confronting a difficult situation. However, that is why we ask for godly wisdom before engaging in the matter. Our hope is not only that we find the wisdom necessary to deal with the issue but that our hearts are prepared to attribute any honor to God.

5. Recognize that others may be better suited to confront someone who is wrong. Sometimes, leaders perceive they must always be at the forefront of every battle, but this is not always the case. Certainly, there will be moments when the responsibility cannot be abdicated to another. However, many situations contain dynamics that would best be suited for someone else to intercede.

For example, a parent may decide that a child's other parent might best speak into a situation concerning a child. Perhaps one parent is coming off a very trying day and does not have the emotional energy to deal with a matter of child discipline. Or perhaps one parent's personality, background, expertise, or experiences might better qualify him or her to address a certain issue with a child.

Similar dynamics may be seen in an organization. God may place in our midst persons who are better equipped and more willing to confront a co-worker for the betterment of the organization. Wisdom in this regard is the better part of valor. Those in leadership must acknowledge that although they are willing, they might not be best suited to confront a particular situation. This decision might extend the tenure of a leader. It might also train and equip other leaders in an organization regarding confrontation. Quite simply, it may just be the best choice for the organization as a whole.

6. Work to be a better listener than a responder. Stephen Covey's book, *The 7 Habits of Highly Effective People*, presents a holistic, integrated, principle-centered approach for solving personal and professional problems. Covey's Habit 5 is built around the principle of seeking first to understand, then to be understood. The words adapt a line from the well-known prayer of St. Francis of Assisi: "Grant that I may not so much seek to be understood, as to understand." Regarding communicating and working through problems with others, Covey writes:

> "Seek first to understand" involves a very deep shift in paradigm. We typically seek first to be understood.

> Most people do not listen with the intent to understand;
> they listen with the intent to reply. They're either
> speaking or preparing to speak. They're filtering
> everything through their own paradigms, reading
> their own autobiography in other people's lives . . .
> That's the case with so many of us. We're filled with
> our own rightness, our own autobiography. We want
> to be understood. Our conversations become collective
> monologues, and we never really understand what's
> going on inside another human being (Covey 2004,
> 239–240).

Covey's words describe most of us as we head into a confrontational setting. Our intent is to clearly make our point and squelch any rebuttals that might be intended. We want to prove we are right; but in doing so, we miss the opportunity to listen and learn. Instead of filtering the discussion through our stories, life experiences, and expectations, we are in a prime position to better understand another person's story and the underlying reason they come from the point of view they do.

Sometimes as we seek to understand and listen, we find a middle ground we never knew existed before. When this happens, the confrontation moves to a win/win for everyone and both parties leave with sense that the good of the whole was accomplished. Other times, situations can be settled by just listening to the concerns of another person. Conflict may pivot on the fact that one person does not feel heard or respected. After being valued enough to be heard and understood, nothing more may be needed.

At its core, listening is a skill that can be learned but must always be intentional. In full disclosure, it is a skill that I have worked diligently on for the past 12 years because I *needed* to work on it. When Covey wrote, "*most* people listen with the intent to reply, not to understand," he was describing me. I am a multi-tasker, always thinking about what I need to do next. Sad to say, that used to be true even when I was talking with someone.

That bad habit changed after a conversation with a young man one Sunday morning after church. After the conversation, I walked over to my wife Ellen, who said, "How's Bob?"

I responded, "He's great. We just had a good conversation." (I thought it was good because I got to say what I needed to, and it didn't take too much time.)

Ellen said, "I think you may have hurt him in the way you closed the conversation and just walked off."

"You think so?"

She said, "Yes, I do. I don't think he finished saying what he wanted to say before you closed up shop." Then she hit me with a zinger of truth: "You do that sometimes when you are tired or super focused on getting a task done. I know you truly care about people, but sometimes you are task-oriented instead, and that hurts folks."

The next Sunday, I intentionally found that young man and said to him, "I need to apologize to you."

He said, "What for?"

"Because I think I may have unintentionally not listened very well to you. I don't want to give you the notion that I don't care about what you have to say. More importantly, I don't want to imply that I don't care about you."

He looked at me for a moment, then sheepishly smiled and said, "I have to admit I did feel that way. I really appreciate your coming back to clear that up."

After that conversation, I tried harder to be an intentional listener. Over time, the journey has made me a better spouse, dad, pastor, friend, and I trust, leader. Ellen will tell you that I have had to be very intentional to change this old habit. Sometimes, I catch myself falling back into the old pattern of seeking to accomplish a task rather than listen, but I continue to work toward becoming a better listener than responder.

7. Do everything to make the conversation clarifying, not cloudy or confusing. Very few people leave a difficult conversation without wishing they had said something more—perhaps made a point more clearly or reached a decision with the other person. This is seldom true of conversations that you have off-the-cuff, for which you do little preparation. Our unfinished business reminds us that it is critical to fulfill the 3 C's of constructive confrontation:

Clear: Make certain that all parties understand what issue necessitated the meeting. It is not a time to chase rabbits or dance around the subject. It is hard to have a productive outcome if there is not clarity regarding the reason and intent for the conversation.

Concise: Before you meet, write down and highlight the salient points you wish to cover. This will keep rambling to a minimum and also make certain that the critical issues are addressed. It is also helpful in making certain that critical points are communicated in the most productive manner. Remember, how we say something is as important as what we say.

Comprehensive: As the conversation proceeds, make sure that both parties are hearing and comprehending the same thing. If not, the parties may reach completely different conclusions. You can check comprehension by periodically asking the question, "Are we hearing the same thing today?" Another comprehension statement would be, "This is what I understand you to be saying..." Then reiterate what you heard. This gives both parties a sense of confidence as they move through the conversation.

It is important to wrap up the meeting by stating what you believe to be the thoughts of everyone concerned. I must confess that I have often omitted this step. Early in my leadership I took for granted that when the discussion was over, everyone was on the same page—only to find out later we were not even reading the same book! When nearing what seems to be the end of the meeting, make your intentions and points clear. In closing, reiterate those points and ask these questions again, "Have we come to the same conclusion today? Do you have any additional questions?" For more serious matters, place the common conclusion in writing and have both parties sign. It is helpful to have written and signed proof of the conclusions reached. Remember, do everything in your power to make the conversation clarifying, not cloudy or confusing.

8. Make certain that grace, mercy, and redemption buffer your actions and words. In every difficult conversation, I try to remember my dad's words, "There is a difference between confronting someone and destroying someone." For justice to be a reality, it must undergird my approach to the conversation, my actions during the conversation, and my words guiding the conversation. It is important that the notions of grace, mercy, and redemption frame my intentions.

Mercy and grace have similar meanings, but the Bible indicates they are different. *Grace* is God's blessing us with what we do not deserve and extending kindness in a way of which we are not worthy. *Mercy* is God's not punishing us as our sins deserve and delivering us from judgment. It is the extension of God's great kindness when condemnation would have been deserved. *Redemption* means to buy out or release someone from their condition of condemnation or servitude. It is the opportunity to have a new beginning.

With those biblically defined thoughts in mind, help both parties find a sense of success at the end of the conversation. If the situation requires you to communicate that a person will no longer have a job, treat the person with more respect than they expected and help them secure a future placement if possible. Your ability to do this may be somewhat limited, but if your intent is to help that person have a sense of success (at least some constructive progress), the potential for good is greater than the potential for destruction. Grace, mercy, and redemption can characterize your conversation, even when you must confront the other person's behavior.

9. Remember that confrontation takes unbelievable energy and focus. Make no mistake, confrontation is an emotionally and physically draining task. Remember this when scheduling your conversation. After Elijah confronted the prophets of Baal, he had to take some much-needed time away (1 Kings 19). God then provided an opportunity for him to eat and sleep. If this is what confrontation does to one of God's all-time spiritual giants, imagine what it does to you and me.

Since confrontation takes a toll, make certain you are rested beforehand and allow time to rest afterwards. It is wise not to have a creative or demanding event immediately following a confrontation—doubly important not to make critical decisions until some emotional, spiritual, and physical renewal has taken place. This will not always be possible, but you often can schedule rest and renewal within reasonable proximity to the conversation.

Remember your Source in times of weariness and struggle, and take time to seek Him out. God's Word invites us to do just that: "I love you, LORD; you are my strength. The LORD is my rock, my fortress, and my savior; my God is my rock, in whom I find protection. He is my shield, the strength of my salvation, and my stronghold. I will call on the LORD, who is worthy of praise, for he saves me from my enemies (Psa. 18:1–3, NLT). Philippians 4:6–7 says, "Do not be anxious about anything, but in everything, by prayer and petition, with thanksgiving, present your requests to God. And the peace of God, which transcends all understanding, will guard your hearts and your minds in Christ Jesus."

Be self-aware in the midst of a confrontation. We all have personal rhythms and personal limitations. Being aware of yours, and making allowances for them, is a key to staying healthy to finish the race set before you.

10. After the confrontation celebrate this fact: We may not be where we wanted to be, but we are one step closer to where we need to be. Very seldom does confrontation end exactly as we desire it to. If it does, throw a party. Celebrate and then take the rest of the day off! However, if it doesn't go exactly as planned or end up where you hoped, remember it is a necessary step to get where you ultimately need to go. The act of confrontation is not the end-all; it is only a step in moving the relationship or organization toward a desired goal. The fact is we can never control how another individual will respond; we can only control how we will respond. No situation is static. There are multiple dynamics at work and countless results are possible. As Robert Burns said, "Even the best laid plans often go awry" (Burns, 1786, 138).

Confrontation is not easy and at times not accomplished in a linear process. But it is a necessary step for any leader, team, or organization to clarify key issues, work through disagreements, determine foundational building blocks, and pursue a mutual vision. Again, I realize confrontation is not the fun part of leadership, whether that be parenting your children or running a Fortune 500 company. But it is a critical part of leadership. We cannot avoid the responsibility simply because we don't enjoy it. Rather than avoid it, we must become better skilled at handling it, both emotionally and in actuality.

When discussing confrontation, I am reminded of a scene in the movie, *Born Again,* about Chuck Colson's life after the Watergate debacle. In the movie, Colson finds himself in prison talking with another inmate whom he praises for being a peace maker. The inmate is somewhat confused over the flattery he has just received because he had just been part of a violent physical confrontation. Then Colson explains the difference between a peace lover and a peace maker. He states, "A peace lover is someone who will go to any length to avoid confrontation. A peace maker is someone who realizes that for there to ultimately be peace, sometimes there must be confrontation."

MANY TIMES, PEACEMAKING ENTAILS CONFRONTING SITUATIONS THAT HINDER THE GOOD OF THE WHOLE.

Most leaders are called to be peace makers, over and over again. This entails confronting situations that hinder the good of the whole. Such situations may be tolerated or overlooked for a time, but ultimately they must be confronted. These situations can be dealt with in a constructive manner if the leader will continuously remember this important fact: There is a difference between confronting a person and destroying a person. If you approach the situation with that thought in mind, you are more likely to handle it in the right way.

Discussion questions

1. By nature, are you a peace lover or peace maker?
2. What fear or inadequacy do you need to overcome to become a peace maker?
3. How are you bettering your skills at confronting?
4. Is there a life situation right now in which you need to confront someone?
5. Who will you consult for advice in how to handle the situation?
6. When will you act regarding this situation?
7. Afterwards, who will debrief with you about how the situation was handled? This will help you to continue growing in your confrontation skills.

14

The Impact of a Few Words

The Power of Thinking before You Speak

IN YEARS PAST, MY CHURCH'S NATIONAL BODY CAME TOGETHER AT AN annual meeting to do the business of the church. A few thousand people were present and Robert's Rules of Order governed the proceedings. We all know people who take these meetings as an opportunity to display their wealth of knowledge and insight regarding Robert's Rules to an extreme extent. (You are thinking of that person right now!)

During one such meeting, a participant was waxing eloquent on some obscure provision of Robert's Rules to make a point that was…pointless. (Now you are really thinking of that person!) Groans throughout the hall expressed everyone's annoyance about the matter. What made matters worse was that the speaker was trying to resolve a situation that involved me.

Finally, I was asked to come forward and verify that the motion would accomplish the intended results. I walked to the podium and flippantly said, "So moved." The audience fell out in laughter and I felt I had made two points. First, the motion was indeed made. Second, I had ended the floor debate as annoying and totally frivolous. I felt very good about my quick wit and the result.

My father was in the assembly that day, and immediately afterwards we shared lunch together. I expected him to compliment me in some way for my actions of the morning. He didn't. He said, "You were a man of few words today."

"I know," I responded. "A few words were enough."

My dad didn't laugh. He simply looked at me and said, "Rolland, sometimes a few words can be the difference between making an enemy or making a friend. Today, I think you probably made an enemy."

I sat back in my chair. I felt angry because of his rebuke, but I also felt embarrassed because I knew he was right. It would have taken no more effort on my part to acknowledge the man's concerns and affirm the need to do things right. Instead, I had played to the crowd. I had an opportunity to lift up another human being, but chose instead to lift myself up and ridicule the other person.

The book of Proverbs contains directives that mirror my father's thoughts that day: "Some people make cutting remarks, but the words of the wise bring healing" (Pro. 12:18). This scripture affirms the power of words to do good or harm. It calls us to consider the needs of another before entering a conversation with or about them.

This was never more evident to me than one night when Ellen and I were watching one of our favorite shows, "The Biggest Loser." One of the finalists was sharing part of her life story and told about the time in middle school that a young boy had called her a fat cow. She began to weep and express the pain those words had caused her. It was evident that the boy's words still brought great pain to this woman, even in her late thirties.

I wish I could say that the occasion in the church assembly was my sole offense in this area; but I cannot. As I look back on my life, I realize that a quick wit and sharp tongue are not always positive attributes. No wonder the Psalmist writes, "I will watch my ways and keep my tongue from sin; I will put a muzzle on my mouth" (Psa. 39:1).

The opportunity to build up or tear down others is presented to us almost on a daily basis. As my father said, most of these situations come down to how we choose to use our words. I have witnessed too many people who have no understanding of the power of their words. Whether it is a mother who constantly finds fault with her children, a husband who never affirms his wife, or a boss who never encourages her employees, much harm can be done with a few words.

WEAPONIZED WORDS TAKE THE LIFE
OUT OF RELATIONSHIPS.

Some of us have learned only too well how to use words in a hurtful manner. In many families, this skill is passed down from generation to generation. In many workplaces, this type of abuse is used as a motivational tool. An environment becomes toxic when this type of negative, critical poison is spewed continuously. Mutual respect and joy are destroyed while apathy and anger find root and grow. In the long run, weaponized words take the life out of relationships and diminish the effectiveness of organizations. As Proverbs 16:24 says, "Pleasant words are a honeycomb, sweet to the soul and healing to the bones."

Many of us have never understood this scripture because this kind of language was seldom shared or modeled for us. Some supervisors never seem to comprehend that employees will work harder if they feel valued for what they do. In team situations, how we say something is as important as what we say. A few words of affirmation, spoken with genuine sincerity, can bring calm to a tense situation and breathe life into a parched and dry relationship. Allow me to offer some suggestions about how to begin doing this in your life.

First, before you speak to another person, ask yourself if the words you are about to say will build up and benefit that individual. As the wise writer of Proverbs said, "Watch your tongue and keep your mouth shut, and you will stay out of trouble" (Prov. 21:23 NLT).

Hitting the pause button is really helpful for those of us with a tendency to be critical and sarcastic. In Oswald Chambers' book, *My Utmost for His Highest,* he makes a statement that has helped guide my life: "When in doubt, wait" (Chambers 1935, 4). If you are about to speak and suspect that your words might not be received well or might create hurt, then don't speak them. Carefully consider how to express yourself in a constructive manner. Just live by the motto, "When in doubt, wait."

One day my wife Ellen and I were sitting in a photographer's waiting room before having our pictures taken. I was thirsty, so I made my way to a water fountain down the hall. When I arrived, a man was cleaning his hairbrush in the water fountain. As you can imagine, my thirst disappeared, replaced with a sense of nausea. I returned to my seat and said to Ellen, "You can't believe what I just saw. A man is cleaning his hairbrush in the water fountain. Can you believe anyone would do that?"

As the man entered the waiting room, a woman sitting beside Ellen leaned forward and asked, "Is that the man?" I nodded affirmatively and she said, "That's my husband."

I simply responded, "Oh. Rest assured he has a clean hairbrush now."

If I had only paused before I had spoken so loudly, perhaps my embarrassment (and Ellen's) would not have been so great. If more of us would learn the value of pausing before we speak, we would do less harm with our critical words. As we saw in the previous chapter, sometimes difficult things must be said. However, they can be said in a way that does not do more harm than good. So pause before you speak. It will enhance your chance of making your words count in a positive way.

Second, ask yourself, does the way I am about to say this match the intent of what I am about to say? Proverbs 13:3 reminds us, "Those who control their tongue will have a long life; opening your mouth can ruin everything" (NLT).

Have you ever said something the wrong way and it ruined everything? That is probably because how you said something didn't match the intent of what you said. This happens quite frequently in marriages, and usually the husband at fault. (At least it often works that way in our marriage!)

One day, early on in our marriage, Ellen and I were working in our yard where a large tree had fallen. I was amazed at how hard Ellen was working and how many of the heavy limbs she had moved to the brush pile. So I turned to her and said, "Ellen, you are a beast!" I meant those words with all the love and affection I had, but Ellen didn't hear my words as being so affectionate!

She was rather quiet the rest of the day. When we went to McDonalds to get a drink to refresh us, I asked if anything was wrong. She simply said, "Do you think 'beast' is the best way to describe me?"

As we made our way through the drive-through, I tried to make sure Ellen understood my intentions. I kept trying to say loving things. So when the waitress handed us our drinks, I said to her, "I love you." To which she replied, "Oh, that's nice. I love you, too." She then gave me my change and closed the window. Ellen and I burst out laughing. Further proof that my intent didn't always match my words!

We have all heard the saying, "How we say something is as important as what we say." Too often, we simply don't think before we speak. In fact, many people are unaware of how their comments damage others because speaking off-the-cuff has just become a way of life.

Third, ask yourself, do your critical comments about others express an inner criticism? "The tongue of the wise makes knowledge appealing, but the mouth of a fool belches out foolishness" (Prov. 15:2 NLT). That verse describes the critical tendency of some people who are inwardly critical of themselves. Their awareness of their own "stuff" burdens them with self-criticism, and that directly influences how they interact with others. To compensate for what they believe are their own inadequacies, they offend others.

Perhaps each of us should take to heart Robert Browning's words: "My business is not to remake myself, but to make the absolute best of what God has made." Please understand that misconceived, negative notions of yourself are not true, nor are they God's assessment of you. We are "fearfully and wonderfully made" (Psa. 139:14) because God has made us. The Hebrew word here translated as *fearfully* means we were not created by chance, but our conception was the conclusion of a holy process, a divine encounter. God Himself reached down and brought Himself to bear in our creation.

The term translated as "wonderfully made" means that it was the result of a delicate and awesome process. It could be said we were hand-woven by God. Therefore, instead of trying to critique what God has wonderfully made, we should celebrate, motivate, and believe in what God has divinely ordered. Our intent and our goal are to make the best out of what God has already blessed.

I was raised in a very close-knit community. We had community picnics and celebrations; in reality, it was a place a lot like the fictional town of Mayberry, N.C. It was such a small community that everyone knew almost everyone else and most families attended the same community events.

The Bird family was one of those families. Joe and Joyce had two children, Steven and Stephanie. You would see the four of them together at most community events.

Everyone knew and loved the Bird family, but especially Stephanie. Stephanie was a special-needs child who had many challenges to overcome daily. Seldom could one drive past the Bird home without seeing one of those parents out in the yard with Stephanie, who would be waving to everyone that came by. This community loved Stephanie in many ways because they saw how this family loved Stephanie.

Years had passed since I connected with the Bird family. I had gone off to college, graduated, and returned home to work. When I stopped at a local restaurant to eat, Mr. Bird saw me and made his way over to my table. We made small talk for a while until I said, "Mr. Bird, how's Stephanie doing?"

When I said those words, his countenance changed and this eyes lit up. It was a wonderful thing to watch this father talk with pride about his daughter. He told me about some of her difficulties and some of the small steps of growth that they had seen in Stephanie. Then he shared some of the great joys she had brought to their lives and how he cherished these moments.

Finally, he paused and said, "You know, Rolland, the way I see it, when God gave Stephanie to Joyce and me, God gave to us a special gift. I believe God thought, *Joe and Joyce will love this special girl in a special way.* So that's what I give my life to everyday. I try to love this special gift in a special way." He paused again, swallowed, and softly began to cry as he said, "Not a day goes by that I don't thank God for her."

Joe Bird had the capacity to see past Stephanie's limitations to appreciate the best in what God had created. Some of us need to do the same for ourselves. We all have issues. We all have flaws. We all have things that we wish we could change about ourselves. But the truth is, our life is a gift from God. Each of us has been uniquely and wonderfully made. We are not perfect people, but God perfectly loves and adores us. We should speak more often of our appreciation for the blessing of our lives instead of being critical of ourselves and others in response to our misconceived notions.

A final suggestion would be to place the following questions in a prominent place and review them before allowing yourself to say things you wish you could take back.

1. Will the words you are about to say build up and benefit that individual?
2. Does the way you're about to say something match the intent of what you are about to say?
3. Do your critical comments about someone else come from an inner criticism?

Tape these questions to your refrigerator door, place them on a bulletin board or by the water cooler at work, use them as a screen saver, keep them on the dash of your car, or use the magnet and stick them on your fridge door. Just do it. You will be amazed at how the tone of your conversations will change as you change the intent and delivery of your words. Your words will begin to change the culture and people around you and even how other people view you.

Recently, that fact was reaffirmed to me in another way. I am privileged to be an adjunct professor for the MBA program at a nearby college. I always open the first session of a course by asking students to introduce themselves by answering four questions: What is your name? What do you do? Why are you here? And what do you hope to gain from the class?

In one new class, students took turns until a young lady that I knew previously responded. She shared her name, told what she did, and then said, "You are the reason that I'm here." I was shocked at her words, but she continued, "Several years ago, I was in a conference at which you spoke. At the close of the session, I shared my hopes and dreams with you, and you encouraged me to pursue my education and work toward my goals." She added, "I have never forgotten your words of encouragement, and I am here today pursuing that goal."

I share this story with great humility, and I wish I could say this happened on a regular basis. But her comment affirmed the power of a few words and how they can make a life-changing difference for another person. I once read that each of us has only so many words that we can use effectively for one day. Why not make each one of them count? And I mean, *really* count.

Let's use our conversations to make friends, not enemies. Let's encourage and build up other human beings, not tear others down. Let's make certain our words become bridges that enable the people who work with us to move toward a better future. Let's create a pattern to intentionally remind our children that God made them and has plans to use them in great ways. Let's use our conversations as launching pads to lift others toward an incredible future. Think about all the good ways we can invest our words!

Ever since that day long ago in the church assembly, I have remembered my father's advice and tried to measure the power of my words and how they will be received by the people with whom they are shared. Dad's assessment of the outcome was probably right. I probably made an enemy and brought needless hurt to that person because I didn't stop to consider the impact of a few words.

Learn from my mistake. Pause and consider the possible impact before you speak. Remember, when in doubt, wait.

Discussion questions

1. Would you define the majority of conversations in your home or workplace as encouraging and affirming?
2. If not, what is the root cause of the negative nature of your conversations?
3. Are these negative conversations creating a toxic culture around you? Is it eroding your relationships with others?
4. When will you utilize the three suggested steps as a family, team, or organization to begin to change the current culture?
5. Who will you ask to coach and hold you accountable through the process?

15

Be Willing to Make Difficult Decisions

The Power of Making Tough Choices

PEOPLE ARE SOMETIMES CALLED TO ASSUME THE OVERWHELMING BURDEN of leadership. They will be asked to say yes or no to specific requests as they take charge. During these moments, it will be up to them to assess if affirming those decisions would benefit the whole in a positive manner. After the assessment, they then offer a final decision on the matter that can alter the future entirely.

Any leader will tell you this is sometimes not the fun part of the job. Invariably, in saying yes or no, the leader will make one person happy and another disgruntled. Over an extended period of time, these heavy decisions can erode a leader's will and energy. An anonymous quote made famous by Hall of Fame football coach Vince Lombardi states, "Fatigue make cowards of us all." (Miller, 2019) If you have led long enough, you know exactly what he meant.

In fact, I remember one Monday morning receiving a phone call from a mentor/friend of mine. He had been in ministry for over forty years and had given leadership to great congregations, as well as holding prominent national positions. He made small talk for a while, which was unlike him, so I asked why he had called me. He answered, "To be honest, I was just sitting here wondering how I would do as a used car salesman, and just wanted to get your thoughts."

I responded, "Tough weekend, huh?"

"You have no idea."

Every leader understands that situation perfectly. We have all had days we want to leave or simply ask God to take this mantle from us.

At a certain point in my life, that statement rang true for me. The job of being a pastor weighed so heavily upon me I contemplated leaving ministry altogether and finding something different to do. That year, we were home in Mississippi for Christmas, visiting my folks. Home visits were normally very relaxing for me because my two sons and I spend a lot of time hunting and enjoying the peace and quiet of the outdoors. The phone never rings and the most difficult decision I make is when to take my nap on the deer stand.

On this particular visit, that was not the case. My workload was so heavy that I had a difficult time escaping from it. At every opportunity, I would tell my father about the problems at our church. During one of those conversations, I was bemoaning certain people who were upset with me over decisions I had made, and told Dad this was wearing me down. I further shared with him I didn't know if I wanted to pastor anymore.

My dad didn't give me much sympathy. He simply said, "Leadership is not for the weak or fainthearted. If you lead, you will always have difficult decisions to make and those decisions will make some people unhappy. Rolland, the truth is that sometimes you have to be a pain in the butt. It's not the fun part, but it is a necessary part of leadership. You'll just have to learn to deal with it."

Dad was a kind man, but he could state the truth in a very pointed manner when he felt it was necessary.

I once heard Bob Russell, long-term pastor of Southeast Christian Church in Louisville, Kentucky, quote President Harry Truman: "If you can't stand the heat, then get out of the kitchen." Under his leadership, the church grew to over fifteen thousand. I am certain he experienced his share of heat in the kitchen.

My father's words and Truman's pointed to the same truth: Sometimes a leader must be the bad guy, the person who makes the difficult decisions and lives with the consequences, even though not everyone approves or likes the choices their leader has made. Leaders will sometimes make decisions that in the short term will alienate some very faithful people, but in the long run will be best for the organization. That is part of the role they hold.

Dr. Henry Cloud in his book, *Integrity*, defines this trait in a leader as a character issue. He writes,

> In some senses, the degree of responsibility, which really is what success is, that someone rises to rests upon their ability and courage to make the difficult calls. And that is not a brain issue, but a character issue. The fortitude to take the heat, the criticism, the rejection, the backs turning on you and maybe never forgiving you for doing what needs to be done, is the issue (Cloud 2006, 155).

Every leader who desires to be effective understands the truth of what my dad stated that day. At one time or another, your decisions will cause you to be seen as the bad guy. This may vary in degrees, based on the consequences of the decision. But like it or not, such a time will come.

This is especially true for a parent. Many parents struggle with this inevitability, because they would rather be their child's friend instead of an authority figure. Sorry, but part of our role as parents is to draw boundaries and determine healthy parameters for our children to function within.

Will this role occasionally anger, frustrate, or disappoint your child? Yes! However, the outcome of not doing this for your child will bring with it much deeper and more detrimental repercussions. Each of us has witnessed children who have never been given boundaries. Their lives are riddled with chaos and conflict because healthy boundaries have never been set. Some parental responsibilities cannot be abdicated. Making tough decisions is one of those.

This is not always easy. In fact, it can be a heavy burden to bear. Listed below are four ways that the burden of leadership can impede the effectiveness of any leader over time. It is important that we are not only aware of these danger zones but intentionally compensate for them.

1. The duration of the struggle can wear leaders out. Sometimes it is not the intensity of the battle but the length of it that wears one down. When our stamina and perseverance wear down, we may not stay the course. Like Elijah in 1 Kings 19, we all have our Jezebels that get under our skin. Their threats cut us repeatedly and, in our weariness, we may run for the mountains instead of staying to face our critics head-on.

In such moments, a leader must have cultivated *integrity*, the kind of leadership that thrives when things are good and stays when things are difficult (Cloud, 31). In extended difficult times, it is crucial that the leader understands his/her emotional rhythm and tank capacity. All of us handle stress differently and find renewal in different ways. Each leader must recognize his/her own pattern and maximize it to stay the long haul. Leadership is a marathon, not a sprint, and marathoners train differently than sprinters do. The same is true for long-term leaders.

2. Leaders must not cut off communication lines and isolate themselves emotionally, spiritually, or relationally. Nothing makes a leader more vulnerable than isolation from those who can support and encourage. Weariness can reach the place that we feel as though we don't have the emotional energy to connect and engage others. When that happens, we are tempted to retreat into ourselves. Counselors refer to this as the turtle response, retreating into our shell for comfort and protection. In truth, this only makes us more vulnerable to the destructive nature of depression and exhaustion, since we have moved away from our support system.

Have you ever watched the hunting tactics of a lion pride on the Discovery Channel? Lions always stalk an animal that is isolated from the herd. Isolation places us in a position of vulnerability. This is why the Bible teaches there is strength in numbers and protection in being connected to others. Remember the passage, "Two people are better off than one, for they can help each other succeed. If one person falls, the other can reach out and help. But someone who falls alone is in real trouble . . . A person standing alone can be attacked and defeated, but two can stand back-to-back and conquer. Three are even better, for a triple-braided cord is not easily broken" (Eccl. 4:9–10, 12, NLT).

During difficult times, be intentional in cultivating points of connection in your life, emotionally, spiritually, and relationally. Each of us needs human connections. These connections do not happen unintentionally, and they are sources of our continued health and well-being.

3. Leaders who receive continual negative and defeating messages may have a crisis of morale. There is no better example of this than Tokyo Rose during the Second World War. She was constantly broadcasting radio messages to try to demoralize our troops. Their best strategy was to tune her out!

If we place ourselves in a position to hear ongoing negative and defeating messages, there's a strong possibility that our hope will diminish. Too many times, we become what we hear most.

I knew a man who pastored a great church. As always, there were some in the congregation who didn't agree with his leadership. He would receive critical letters from a particular group on a regular basis. On Sunday mornings, this group would sit directly in front of him while he taught. The dour looks on their faces sent a barrage of negative messages while this man was preaching. Remember, negative messages can be both verbal and visual.

Then one Sunday he noticed something. A wonderful couple that loved the pastor positioned themselves two rows behind the critical group and began sitting there every Sunday. During the service, their faces radiated smiles that spoke support and love. In a short time, the pastor taught himself to look above the critical group and focus on the support of the other couple. It wasn't long before the smiles of one couple rose above the frowns of the other group.

In many ways, that is what leaders have to do. All leaders have critics and those who wish to demoralize. The key is to listen to the negative but not allow the ongoing defeatist messages to take life from us. By staying connected with those who give us life and maintaining relationships that infuse us with hope and purpose, we can rise to the challenge. Look above the fray. Concentrate on the good that is being done and the good people enabling it to happen. Listen and learn from your critics, but don't allow the undertow of criticism to pull you under.

4. Weariness can make us vulnerable to one overwhelming blow. In 1990, before our troops entered Desert Storm, the Joint Forces dropped tons and tons of bombs in the vicinity of the enemy forces. Our intent was to send an overwhelming message: You are defeated before you begin. Sometimes, in the midst of great struggles, we can think the same way about what lies before us. If that is the case, we may quit before the battle begins.

Please know, every leader must have an abiding desire to make a difference for good. Allow that desire for the greater good to overcome your ego and need for control. Great leaders are rare breeds. They are not those who wish they could do something; they are the ones God has gifted to make something happen. As I have watched great leaders like that, their leadership is always devoted to advancing the greater good.

Certainly, opposition can create barriers to hinder those who are trying to accomplish something good. In fact, opponents may work to erect so many barriers that the leader simply quits. This happens more often than we wish.

When I turned fifty, Ellen and I ran a marathon—26.2 miles. It took us nine months to train for the event. Even though we read about marathons and gained wisdom from those who had run multiple marathons, the biggest lesson we learned was that the real marathon starts at mile marker 20!

At twenty miles, fatigue really starts to set in and your body wants to shut down. Your body has, for lack of a better word, governors that help to regulate it. Those governors enable your body to function within healthy limits. At twenty miles, your body begins to respond to sustained physical stress. Red lights begin to flash, warning signals go off, and your body makes perfectly clear that you have exceeded the limits of "normal." At the 20-mile marker, your body begins to send out S.O.S. distress signals that scream, "May Day, May Day!" Any marathoner has to make a critical decision at this point: whether to quit or finish the race.

All around Ellen and me were people who thought toward quitting. Some were sitting on curbs, some stretched out on lawns; all of our bodies were screaming for us to drop out of the race. Then Ellen and I saw the most remarkable thing.

Other people, who had previously run marathons, began to slow and encourage those who had stopped running. They knew this was when these folks most needed encouragement and support. We watched as experienced runners reached down to help novice runners off the curb with encouraging words and a few "trade secrets."

One of those secrets shared with us was to set a smaller goal to work toward. I know this sounds crazy, but at that point that Ellen and I started concentrating on catching one particular person in blue shorts who was ahead of us. We decided quit thinking about our fatigue and started another race for the final 6.2 miles. We were going to catch "old blue shorts" before we reached the finish line!

We trudged our way to Mile 24. I say "trudged" because we had not run gracefully since Mile 8! Honestly, I don't think we ever did run what you might call gracefully! We trudged, waddled, walked, wandered, and wobbled to Mile 24. There a particularly nice and encouraging man was handing out water. No doubt he could see the pain and exhaustion on our faces, so besides handing us water, he also ran with us for a short distance. Then he said in a very upbeat manner, "You have just run 24 miles! Less than 1 percent of the entire population of the world has ever done so. You only have 2.2 miles left to finish this race and accomplish something mind-boggling. You can wrestle an alligator for 2.2 miles! Now go, finish this race!"

I don't know how many alligators he had wrestled, but his words inspired us. We picked up our pace to a crawl and made our way forward. We came over the next hill and a man had speakers the size of round hay bales sitting in his front yard. He was blaring to unknown decibels the theme song to the movie, *Chariots of Fire*. We threw our heads back like Eric Liddell and made our way to the final stretch, all the while keeping our eyes on "old blue shorts."

During the final half mile, another wonderful thing happened. Our two sons came out of the crowd and ran beside us, speaking words of encouragement all the way to the finish line! When we crossed that line, it was an emotional and glorious moment! We had accomplished something that most people find impossible, and we did it with the people we loved the most. (By the way, we caught up to "old blue shorts"!)

FOCUS YOUR TIME AND ENERGY ON THOSE WHO GIVE LIFE, NOT THOSE WHO TAKE IT FROM YOU.

Leaders will always have a reason to quit, but God needs you to finish for the greater good! He has gifted you to make a difference and He needs you to accomplish the good He has set before you. It means that you need to keep yourself healthy emotionally, spiritually, relationally, and physically. Focus your time and energy on those who give life, not those who take it. That is your right and a necessary step to finishing the race God has called you to.

I came to that realization during the conversation with my dad that day I asked his advice about troubles at the church. I realized that if I desired to do more than just exist in my leadership position, I would have to recondition myself in transformative ways. The journey has not always been easy because I am a people-pleaser and I want others to like me. Therefore, the following steps took time, great emotional effort, and great support from my wife, family, and other key leaders in my life.

I first had to recondition the way I found affirmation. I was naïve enough to think that when I made big decisions, people would rise and cheer. After all, I had been raised in a home of great support, I was a likeable guy, and I thought everyone would love my leadership. I needed to understand that popularity does not equal leadership, so my need to be liked would not always be realized in a leadership role. In truth, I came to understand that there would be moments when people would walk away, disgruntled and angry. If I was truly functioning as the leader God called me to be, then a part of my job would be to make difficult calls and learn to live with the consequences. I had to make decisions for the benefit of the whole, and my being liked was secondary to that.

I also had to recondition how I responded to criticism. Instead of allowing it to emotionally drain me for hours, I had to learn some coping techniques to offset my people-pleasing needs. I was coming to the hard, cold fact that criticism is a part of a leader's life.

Boxers understand when they climb into the ring there is a high probability of forceful, painful contact with their opponents. Likewise, leaders will take their share of blows that knock the wind out of them if they lead long enough. That is why boxers do so much abdominal and core work. They expect to get hit. In the same way, leaders have to toughen up and condition themselves to expect criticism and take some hits.

We also must grow to understand that some decisions deserve criticism. We all wish we were always right, all of the time, but that is simply not the case. We will make some poor decisions, at least decisions not made with the best timing and finesse. In those moments, we must accept the criticism along with the praise and be ready to offer an apology where it is needed. If you desire to be perfect and bat 1,000 percent, then don't become a leader. Hall of Famers only hit around 300.

I also had to learn what my emotional rhythm was. All of us have a rhythm in which we function best. Some of us take criticism in stride. In fact, they enjoy it. I have a friend like that. Someone once said of him, "Conflict for James is recreation." That was not true for me. Therefore, I had to learn what emotional rhythm gave me the best opportunity to recover from the energy drain that conflict and criticism brought. I learned that I needed to recognize the signs of extreme fatigue and respond with some time away or plan an activity that gave me life.

I learned to schedule time around people who gave me life instead of people that drained life from me. I had to understand it was OK not to say yes to everyone who desired to meet with me, especially at critical (no pun intended) moments. This does not mean that I never meet with those who disagree with me or criticize me; that would lead to even more conflict. However, I can interact on a regular basis with those who cause me to laugh and give me joy. Laughter and joy are often the best medicine for fatigue and weariness.

Another point of growth for me was in the emotional arena. I had to open up to others regarding difficult scenarios I was passing through. That thought may trouble you. You may not see yourself being vulnerable and open to others, especially about your struggles and hurts. You may believe a leader never shows weakness and must give the impression of being invincible. Believe me, I can understand this mindset because I once held the same misconceived notion. However, I finally came to understand the wisdom the Bible shares about this.

For too long in my life I did not understand the wisdom of reaching out to gain strength from others. Therefore, when I got knocked down, I asked no one to help pick me up. I isolated myself from true friendships that expected me to be real and vulnerable. In the words of Ecclesiastes 4, my leadership style was to isolate myself when I faced real trouble. In hindsight, this was due to arrogance and pride. The Bible makes clear that these can be our biggest hindrance to wholeness. Scripture says, "Human pride will be humbled, and human arrogance will be brought down" (Isa. 2:17 NLT). "Pride leads to disgrace, but with humility comes wisdom" (Prov. 11:2 NLT). "But those who exalt themselves will be humbled, and those who humble themselves will be exalted" (Matt. 23:12 NLT).

It doesn't take a rocket scientist to deduct the formula for personal ruin and failure:

Weariness + Isolation + Vulnerable = Real Trouble

This new awareness called me to cultivate relationships with three men that I trusted unequivocally. I shared with them every other week and it was understood that everything said was in complete confidence. After a time of building trust, I began to share my struggles, hurts, and failures. It was one of the most strengthening and life-giving things I have ever done. Trust me, we laughed more than we discussed heavy issues. However, during times of intense criticism, they picked me up and dusted me off with encouragement. Other times, they told me to quit feeling sorry for myself and move on. In every case, they were examples of true friends. And the best part, I was not isolated or trying to do it all alone anymore.

Finally, I had to cultivate a mindset of "deal with it and stay the course." Sometimes issues cannot be avoided or overlooked; they must be confronted and resolved for the good of the whole. At other times, the issue is minimal and little time is needed to resolve the problem. At still other times, the problem is more significant and the recovery is extended. This is when weariness can take its toll.

This is when a leader must build up the stamina and resolve needed to stay the course. It is also here that a leader needs total dependency on Someone bigger. Psalm 18 is a part of God's Word that I have on speed-dial during this type of season. Remember Chambers' words: "Sometimes there is even nothing to obey, the only thing we must do is to maintain a vital connection with Jesus Christ, to see that nothing interferes with that" (Chambers, 85). This is why the psalmist prayed, "I love you, Lord; you are my strength. The Lord is my rock, my fortress, and my savior; my God is my rock, in whom I find protection. He is my shield, the power that saves me, and my place of safety" (Psa. 18:1–2, NLT).

When I played high school football, every Wednesday we would run twenty 100-yard belly slams. That meant that while we were running 100 yards, the coach's whistle would blow every five yards and we would dive on our bellies, only to get up and do it again five yards later. The coach told us that no team would be as well-conditioned as we were and, when other teams were ready to quit in the fourth quarter, we would be conditioned to handle the fatigue.

In many ways, leaders have to condition and recondition themselves to handle the fatigue of leadership. Like the twenty 100-yard belly slams, this is often not fun, easy, or attractive; but it is necessary to thrive in the good times and stay in the difficult ones.

Leaders are called to deal with tough decisions and criticism. In doing so, a leader may have to be a part of difficult decisions. It is a part of being a leader, but it does not have to be the part that defeats you. We can learn to deal with criticism and problems—not always enjoy them, but deal with them. Every person has an emotional rhythm and can discern a healthy emotional pattern to put into practice. We can learn to cultivate friendships that give us energy and support. Over time, we can cultivate a mindset that is determined to deal with the conflict and stay the course. Each of these steps is critical because together they help form a much healthier way to walk the journey of leadership. This is especially true when you occasionally have to be the bad guy who makes tough decisions.

Discussion Questions

1. Are you able to make difficult decisions in your leadership role? If not, why?
2. How do the consequences of those decisions affect you?
3. If they affect you negatively, what coping techniques do you need to cultivate to better handle those moments?
4. Are there any areas of your life in which you are abdicating responsibility and not making tough decisions?
5. Are you hurting someone else by abdicating your responsibility?
6. How will you take ownership of those responsibilities in the future?

16 CHAPTER

Work as Hard as You Know How, Be as Honest as You Can Be, Then Sleep Well at Night

The Power of Honesty

AT ONE TIME OR ANOTHER, EVERYONE FEELS STRESSED AND OVERLOADED, as we have discussed in previous chapters. We all know the feeling of "having too many irons in the fire," "not enough time in the day," and "meeting ourselves coming and going." The list of slogans could go on and on, but you get the gist. For most of us, this just seems to be the way we live our lives.

The crucial question is this: Will we allow an unbalanced pace to consume us, dominate us, and take life from us? All of us have read statistics regarding the fact that stress raises our blood pressure, incites heart problems, and causes depression. There is no doubt that continued stress affects our well-being.

At one point in my life, this pattern of excessive busyness was becoming the norm for me. At the church I was then pastoring, my additional responsibilities were building a new multi-purpose facility, leading a fundraising campaign, serving on two boards outside the church, coaching a Little League baseball team, speaking to various groups across the country, and trying to be a great father and husband to a busy family.

One day while my mom and dad were visiting, Dad shared his concern that my schedule was affecting me physically. He then asked me two very pointed questions: "Why do you feel the need to do so many things?" and, "Do you feel the need to impress others?"

I wanted to deny the accusation implied by the latter question, so I gave a vague answer as to how this was just a busy season of life, our schedule would slow down in the near future, and things would be better. But deep inside, I knew my dad had driven right straight to the heart of the problem with his simple questions. In fact, they forced me to realize that most of what I did was in direct response to how people would view me.

QUIT WORRYING ABOUT WHAT EVERYONE ELSE THINKS.

Over the next few days, I wrestled with this personality trait and the hold it had over me. As their visit continued, I had another personal conversation with my dad. He shared how, at one time in his life, he had reached a point of such sheer exhaustion that he would come home from work at 5:30 in the afternoon and go straight to bed. He did not even have the energy to interact his family. I said that sounded familiar. At any moment, I felt all the plates I was spinning could come crashing down. Then I asked him how he overcame that difficult time in his life.

He said that first, he went to his doctor and had a thorough physical. Second, he heeded his doctor's advice and found ways to relax and get away from the constant grind. Third, he adopted a new motto and lived with it. His new motto was to work as hard as you know how, be as honest as you can be, and then sleep well at night. "Basically," he said, "I quit worrying about what everyone else thought."

Those words spoke strongly to my heart and psyche that day. For many years, I kept these words as the screen saver on my computer.

On days when the people pleaser in me would raise its ugly head, these words reminded me that I worked and played only to an audience of One.

Jesus said, "There's trouble ahead when you live only for the approval of others, saying what flatters them, doing what indulges them" (Luke 6:26, The Message). The trouble is when this verse describes the life you're living; you will feel you never measure up, nor will you reach any sane sense of personal fulfillment. There will always be the next task, the next opportunity, the next this or the next that to conquer. If we live for others, we will never reach contentment in ourselves. No matter how hard we try, we are incapable of arriving. We will always be traveling the wrong road because it is a road dictated to us by the need for the approval of others. It will never lead us to the place of personal fulfillment and contentment.

My life was living evidence of this truth. I was not driven by what truly needed to be done, but what I thought others thought needed to be done. The healthy road, the fulfilling road I sought, was currently not entered in my GPS. My life was out of balance and I needed to make some changes. So I began to work on the three areas that my dad's motto gave me.

First, I took to heart the notion that I needed to focus on things that needed my attention and effort. This meant prioritizing my schedule in a way that focused my time and energy on "must do" items. This forced me make hard choices about what and when things needed to be done. It was amazing how this process filtered through the many voices that had called out for my time before.

About this time, I encountered Steven Covey's book, *First Things First,* and began to determine the True North Principles that would define my life and how I would respond to what Covey refers to as the moment between stimuli and response. Over time, my schedule began to change and my effectiveness began to rise. My stress level lowered as my decisions were based more on priorities, values, and principles rather than other's perceptions and preferences.

Second, I began to evaluate my honesty in regard to others and myself. Doing this forced me to ask if I was doing something or saying something because of my need to please others or because it was something legitimate that would be fruitful and beneficial. I took this a step further by asking others heavily invested in me to share their opinions about what should be a priority in my life and what should not. Many refer to this as a 360-degree assessment of your life. I say: Ask people who know and matter to you to speak into your life. Proverbs 16:13 points to this kind of peer assessment when it says, "The king is pleased with words from righteous lips; he loves those who speak honestly" (NLT).

Friends and family who speak truth to each other are invaluable assets. Developing those relationships is healthy, necessary, and productive. With added insight and wisdom from those people, the tangents that had once consumed my time were quickly placed on the sidelines and were replaced by functions that worked within my giftedness. This made a personal and professional difference. In fact, I believe I finally began to give an *honest* day's work as it pertained to effectiveness and fulfillment.

A third aspect of this process was being as honest as I could. This might sound trite, but being honest means learning to be honest with yourself and others by sharing truthful opinions and thoughts. People pleasers have a tendency not to share what they feel, for fear of upsetting the apple cart or causing someone not to like them. For me, it was probably a little of both, which meant I wasn't being the true me.

During this time of struggle, I was reading John Eldredge's book, *Wild at Heart,* in which he recounts the time a friend made this suggestion: "Let people feel the weight of who you are and let them deal with it" (Eldredge 2010, 151). When I read these words, I couldn't move past them. It was as if someone had taken a scope and was viewing a part of my heart that few people ever saw. It was the part of me that held back my deep, true feelings from most people; therefore, I was cheating myself and them. I meditated on the consequences of placing too much importance on how others viewed my thoughts and actions. One consequence was the compulsion to own much more than I needed to have.

This was a turning point for me, as I determined to be true to myself and others. People could start carrying their own weight; I was tired of doing that for them. This principle brought a newfound peace and contentment to my life. I felt more relaxed with who I was and who I wasn't. When deep-seated honesty replaces deep-seated angst, the need for outward approval diminishes greatly. I was freed as grace began to replace my critical nature of myself. All perfectionists are critical of themselves. I was no exception. I began to give myself more grace and also began to give others more grace if they disagreed with me. The criticism was now their problem, not mine. I could offer them grace to disagree or dislike me, but I no longer carried their baggage.

Perhaps for the first time, I began to understand and take a hold of the words found in 1 John 4:18, "Such love has no fear, because perfect love expels all fear. If we are afraid, it is for fear of punishment, and this shows that we have not fully experienced his perfect love" (NLT).

The reality hit me that God's perfect love did not depend on my perfection. In fact, imperfections are why grace is necessary and why God offers it in abundant proportions. Trust me when I speak of the need for abundant proportions! I had never really given grace to myself by allowing others to deal with me as I was. Suddenly, God's complete and perfect love overcame my fears and imperfections in a way that freed me to be me. I progressed to the place of allowing others to feel the weight of who I was and being OK with doing so.

Finally, I made it a priority to release and relax. Daily I made a conscious effort to release things I could not control and quit obsessing over them. I took to heart Jesus' words in Matthew 6:27, "Who of you by worrying can add a single hour to his life?"

My life made it perfectly clear that I had not produced anything significant in all my worrying. Most people find this to be true. My poor results were not from lack of effort. Obsessive efforts had become so ingrained in me that I had to do something to break the cycle. The Bible instructs us to "be transformed by the renewing of our minds (Rom. 12:2)," and this transformation takes time and effort. We did not learn the pattern overnight and we won't overcome it overnight, but it *can* be overcome.

Scripture encourages us to begin focusing on "things that are true, noble, right, pure, lovely, admirable, excellent or praiseworthy" (Phil. 4:8). In essence, we are to begin replacing that which hurts and obsesses us with that which heals and releases us. I began to keep on my desk a stack of note cards with quotes and scripture quotations. At certain moments, I would read those cards and began to replace my worry with their words of assurance and strength. I was amazed at the peace, strength, and contentment this process began to bring into my life. It was not instantaneous, but a gradual transition and the process continues today.

Sad to say, in many ways at that point in my life, I could not relate to Isaiah 51: 11, which states, "Gladness and joy will overtake them, and sorrow and sighing will flee away." Gladness and joy would not have described my approach to ministry at the time, but sorrow and sighing were predominant. Even so, in his infinite strength and mercy, God began to change that within me.

At that point, Ellen and I created a motto of our own that we live by even today: *Never let 'em steal your joy.* Please know there are situations and people that have the capacity to take joy from you. I honestly believe that some people see their capacity to criticize as their spiritual gift and desire to share that gift with others. Whether others desire to receive that "gift" or not is not really their concern. They are simply gift-givers and feel called to share their depressing opinions on a regular basis.

Since that time, we have made a united effort that take hold of joy and gladness and make them a regular part of our lives. We have come to understand that we might listen to certain opinions, but we don't have to carry them with us. We can simply choose to leave behind whatever has the capacity to steal our joy. One of the habits we have cultivated is before we kiss and say goodbye to each other every morning, we say, "Laugh a lot today." This is our daily reminder that joy is not to be taken for granted and we must intentionally cultivate and protect it in our lives.

We have also determined to limit the opportunities that we give others to steal joy from us. Whether we realize it or not, we cannot afford to take this choice lightly. All of us have a certain allotment of energy in one day. If we choose to consistently allow life-takers to dominate us, then our tanks will be depleted when good things come upon us. It is a simple matter of supply and demand, and we must make time for more supply than demand.

A final necessary step in this process was learning how to teach myself to play. My task-driven nature left me feeling guilty when I did something just for fun. That was a pattern I realized I needed to break. Therefore, during this difficult season, Ellen and I decided to run the marathon mentioned in the previous chapter. Ellen knew it was a long-term goal that I had set years before and she suggested we go for it! To accomplish this task, we began a training program that lasted for nine months.

As I look back, this marathon was one of our saving graces during a difficult time. For the times we were training, we talked, hurt, laughed, hurt, processed, hurt, and accomplished something that at the beginning seemed impossible. It was not only an incredible physical journey, but an incredible spiritual journey as well. Ever since that time, regular exercise has been a consistent part of our lives.

I have begun to play golf on a more regular basis with Ellen, my sons, and friends. I have learned that these times are incredibly important times of rest and renewal. The truth is, everyone needs some fun and relaxation in their lives, but this only happens when we make that choice.

Now I was ready to experience my father's final piece of his motto. I would go to sleep and rest well at night. In doing so, I began to focus on what Andrew Murray called "enough grace" for a day. He writes,

> As a child easily masters the lessons in a book when each day he is only given one lesson to learn, but would be utterly hopeless if the whole book were given him at once, so it would be with man if there were no divisions of time. Broken small and divided into fragments, he can bear them; only the care and work of each day have to be undertaken – the day's portion in its day. The rest

> of the night fits him for making a fresh start with each
> new morning; the mistakes of the past can be avoided
> and its lessons improved. (Murray 1979, 112).

I began to see each night as an opportunity "for making a fresh start for each new morning," instead of an opportunity to rehash and critique my mistakes and inadequacies. I know it sounds peculiar to some, but for those who currently share that unbalanced, perfectionist approach to life, this statement makes perfect sense.

I began to learn how to take deep, restful breaths and go to sleep. I also began to learn how to put aside the things that preoccupied me and learn to live with enough grace for a day. Over time, this has brought a deep-seated peace and contentment to my life. Is my life perfect? No. Do I still have times of worrying about what others think? Yes. But now they are fleeting moments instead of moments that consume me.

In reflection, I believe that this new centeredness is found in two things. First, understanding that I do what I do for an audience of One, and One only. I will not falter from that sacred reality. Second, I seek to give myself totally to the people and efforts that matter most. It is amazing what a freeing factor this is. There are no worries about "could I," "should I," or "would I," only the deep sense that all I can do is all I can do, and the rest is left to Someone much bigger than me. Giving one's best to the right things makes the best difference in one's life.

I love the game of baseball. My love affair with the game has existed as long as I can remember. In fact, I grew up in an era and place that allowed me, as a pre-teen, to ride my bicycle several miles to the ballfield and play baseball daily with my friends. Some days, we would play all day. My mom would give me a quarter. For lunch, the entire gang would walk to McPhail's Grocery and buy a Coke and a Honey Bun and still have a few cents for some Super Bubble bubble gum. (Sorry, no other bubble gum would suffice. It was Super Bubble or bust.)

Over those years of elementary, middle school, and high school, I played with and against the same group of guys. We were teammates for practice, enemies on game day, and best friends for life. But there was another trait that we shared. We were good at baseball. At the age of 15, our All-Star team won the State Babe Ruth Championship and got to play in the regional Babe Ruth World Series. Not too shabby for a bunch of country boys from Mississippi!

In high school, our success continued. My senior year, our team was undefeated and headed for the state playoffs. In the playoffs we were matched against Iuka High School who had a great team. They were led by a great player named Don Robinson. Robinson went on to pitch at Mississippi State and was later drafted by the Houston Astros. In the first of a three-game series, we went to Iuka's home field and Robinson shut us down. We have all heard the statement, "Great pitching shuts down great hitting." That was certainly the case for us that time.

The second game found us at home and feeling good about our chances. It was a great game, tied as we entered the final innings. I was in left field, my usual position. With two runners on, a fly ball was hit to deep left field. I drifted back to the fence as I had done so many times. This was the field I had grown up on. The same field which I rode my bike to in order to play while in elementary school. I knew this field like the back of my hand.

But that was not the case on this day. We had torrential rains the day before the game and the water had washed away some sand right by the fence. As I drifted back, placed my hand on the fence to get my bearings, my foot hit the indention caused by the rain and it dropped the top of my glove by an inch or two; enough that the ball tipped off my glove and went over the fence. Iuka went on to win that game and the State championship.

Needless to say, we were crushed as a team. Especially me. I had made that catch a hundred times over my years of playing; but on that day, missing that ball cost us the game. I sat in the dugout until only a few of us players were left. It was then I saw my dad. He had come back to the field and made his way beside me on the dugout bench. For the longest time, we didn't say a word. Then I turned to him and said, "Dad, I can't believe I missed that ball. I still can't believe I missed it."

He paused a moment, then looked at me and said, "I only have one question for you. Did you give your best?"

I responded, "Dad, you know I always give my best."

With that, he reached over and patted my leg, "Then I think you won, Son. I think you won."

THE KEY TO LIVING WITH ENOUGH GRACE FOR
THE DAY IS TO GIVE YOURSELF GRACE.

My dad understood that giving your best has the potential to free a person from most regrets. When you give your best, you don't have to stay focused on the rearview mirror. You can take pride in your effort and be content that all you can do, is all you can do. Then you don't have to carry the weight of others or worry about what others think. You can learn how to put the wrong things aside and live with enough grace for the day. You can take hold of joy and gladness and make them a regular part of your life.

The key to living with enough grace for the day is to learn to give oneself grace. I remember the day I began to understand the concept of grace in a personal manner. As a pastor, I had taught about it and encouraged others to experience it, but I am not certain I had ever really personalized it. Grace receiving is an area most perfectionists wrestle with.

I shared earlier that our oldest son, Tyler, was born with spina bifida. On the day of his birth, a team came from an outstanding children's hospital to evaluate Tyler and the doctors had given us the overview of what they thought Ty's medical prognosis was before they transferred him to the larger hospital with the specialty spina bifida clinic. It was not what first-time parents wanted to hear.

I had a few moments to spend with Tyler before they transferred him to the specialty children's hospital. He was alone in a room, lying on an examination table. He was wrapped in a blanket and his breathing was more gasping instead of steady breaths. I looked down at his feet. It was clear that his left foot and ankle had complications. I wondered to myself if those feet would ever be put to the use that had been intended. Yet at that moment, my overarching concern was that our son would simply live.

I knelt beside that table and took his little feet in my hands. I began to cry out to God that I didn't care if he was perfect. I only cared that he lived. I promised God that no matter what struggles came and no matter the imperfections or limitations Tyler might have, we would love him completely and without reservation. No matter what.

At that moment, the Lord spoke to my heart and said, "Rolland, that is exactly how I love you. Even with your imperfections, your brokenness, your hurts, I love you endlessly and without reservation." It's crazy to think that in one of the most difficult and painful moments in my life, God began the process of making me a grace giver and a grace receiver.

Over the 34 years since that day, I have come to understand that grace always stands strongest in brokenness because those moments always bring with them our greatest need for receiving grace. I have also come to understand that it is impossible to give away what one does not give to one's self. The apostle Paul had the same kind of revelation as the Lord spoke to him regarding his own imperfections and limitations: "My grace is sufficient for you, for my power is made perfect in weakness. Therefore, I will boast all the more gladly about my weaknesses, so that Christ's power may rest on me" (2 Cor. 12:9).

May this be that kind of turning point in your life as you learn the important lesson of receiving and giving yourself enough grace for the day. Your imperfections and brokenness will never hinder God's ability to cover them with His unlimited and unending love and grace. Learn this lesson and, as you do, begin making it a reality in the way you love yourself and others. Then take my dad's advice and work as hard as you know how, be as honest as you can be, and then sleep well at night. That trilogy has the making of a wonderful life that matters.

Discussion questions

1. Are you honest with yourself and others on a regular basis?
2. Will you allow people to feel the weight of who you are and allow them to deal with it?
3. What personal issues keep you from saying "yes" to the first two questions?
4. Do you know and experience the freedom of giving your best?
5. Do you believe God has enough grace to cover you every day?
6. Do you live like He does?

17

CHAPTER

Sometimes All People Need is a Second Chance

The Power of Redemption

IT WAS EARLY AFTERNOON ON A SATURDAY AND MY DAD ASKED ME TO RIDE with him to visit some people. I was probably 13–14 years old and really hated for my Saturday to be interrupted. I asked him why we were going, and he simply said there was a family who was struggling and he had some work to offer the man. I was not that enthused and reluctantly climbed into my dad's truck. It only took about 10–15 minutes to drive to their house. When we arrived, the home was not too much to look at and you could tell the family was struggling. The wood was well-worn and the paint almost completely gone. Dad put the car in park and asked me to stay in the car while he talked with the father.

As Dad knocked on the door, the man stepped out onto what had one time been a porch. When he did, I recognized the man and knew who the family was immediately. They talked for about twenty minutes, then shook hands and Dad made his way back to the car. He dropped into the seat beside me, sighed, and said, "Son, sometimes all people need is a second chance." With that he cranked the engine on the truck, and we headed for home.

But my mind was still fixed on the family I had just seen. To be honest, I was embarrassed for how I had acted at school the day before. You see, I had made fun of the family's youngest daughter for how she was dressed. I did not know her family's situation; I only knew that her clothes were not what the in-crowd wore. Now I sat beside my father, ashamed of my behavior. All I could hear were his words, "Sometimes all people need is a second chance." His words of grace and hope condemned my words and actions of judgement and criticism.

I am thankful God is all about second chances. After reading many of the previous scenarios, it is easy to ascertain I have needed second chances on more than one occasion. In fact, I have come to deeply appreciate this aspect of what the Good News of grace and redemption is all about. God is all about giving to you and me what our actions really don't deserve and that is a second chance with Him and with others. We all love stories about the underdog who gets a second chance and overcomes the miscues or tragedy of the past.

The movie *Hoosiers* tells the Cinderella story of a small-town Indiana high school basketball team that wins the state championship. One important character, an alcoholic named Shooter, played by Dennis Hopper, has failed at most things in his life—but he has an extraordinary knowledge of and passion for the game of basketball.

The coach, played by Gene Hackman, works with Shooter to give him a second chance. He does so by asking Shooter to be his assistant coach and soon Shooter is on the bench. The little-known Hickory High School basketball team is starting to experience winning ways when the coach decides to get himself thrown out of a pivotal game. He pulls the referee aside and says, "Kick me out of the game." The ref doesn't know what the coach is up to, but he tosses him out of the game.

Shooter is terrified. A few scenes earlier, after a drinking binge, Shooter promised the coach he'd stay sober and remain as the assistant on one condition: "You've got to give me your word," said Shooter, "that you will not be kicked out of no games!"

The game is in the final seconds and the score is tied. The Hickory players call a time out. In the team huddle, all eyes are on Shooter, including his son's, who never thought his dad should be in this position in the first place.

Shooter is paralyzed by fear. He can't speak. Finally, his son says, "You reckon Number Four will put up their last shot, Dad?" That seems to jump-start Shooter, and he haltingly calls a play. The team goes back on the floor and begins to execute it when Shooter calls another time out.

Now he is completely engaged in the game, and his knowledge and passion for basketball have overtaken his fear. He lays out the strategy for the next play with confidence; "All right, now listen to me. This is the last shot that we got. All right? We're gonna run the picket fence at 'em. Merle, you're the swing man. Jimmy, you're solo right. All right, Merle should be open, swinging around the end of that fence. Now boys, don't get caught watchin' that paint dry!"

The players are with him. They walk back onto the floor, run the play to perfection, and sink the game-winning basket. Of course, Shooter and the players are deliriously happy. Amid the celebration, Shooter's son looks into his father's eyes and says, "You did good, Pop. You did real good."

A weak, shame-filled man "did real good" because someone decided he was worth a second chance. Interesting to note, that the coach who gave him the second chance was a person who was experiencing the same opportunity. In the same way, God sees our value and loves us enough to take a second chance on us. The Bible is filled with examples of this truth. The parable of the prodigal son is all about a father's second chance for a wayward son (Luke 15:11–32). The story of Jesus' restoring Peter is about a second chance after he has deserted and denied him (John 21:15–19). The story of a common criminal calling out to Jesus for mercy on a cross is about second chances as Jesus tells him, "Today, you will be with me in paradise" (Luke 23:43).

Please know that God is all about second chances; it is what the story of the Cross is built upon. Sometimes life through God's providence gives to you and me an unbelievable gift, the gift of a second chance.

It is a gift that we can graciously give or receive. The hope would be that this second chance is lived out to the fullest potential.

> **A chance to restore a broken relationship we thought was lost forever.**
> **A chance to right a wrong from the past that has haunted us over time.**
> **A chance to pursue a dream we thought would never be reached.**

Yes, life does have second chances. But here's the catch: Being given a second chance and taking advantage of a second chance are two very different things. To take advantage of a second chance requires us to be sensitive to and aware of several dynamics at work.

The life of Moses in Exodus 2–3 is a perfect example of this. Moses was raised in a life of privilege. Adopted as a baby by Pharaoh's daughter, he was raised in Pharaoh's court, ate the finest foods, was taught by the world's greatest scholars, and lived a life of luxury. His only problem was that he had everything but couldn't control himself. The result was his temper got the best of him and ended up killing a man. In response to his crime, he fled Egypt and made his way to Midian, where he married into a family of sheep herders. There Moses, the foster son of Pharaoh, settled into his position of guiding and caring for stinky sheep. For forty years, this task was a precursor to what lie ahead.

God wasn't done with Moses. In fact, unbeknownst to him, God was about to use all of his life, the good and the bad, as preparation for what a second chance would have to offer.

In the Bible and in life, second chances have some common characteristics. The first one is this: Second chances are often preceded by God's getting our attention. "Moses led the flock far into the wilderness and came to Sinai, the mountain of God. There the angel of the LORD appeared to him in a blazing fire from the middle of a bush. Moses stared in amazement. Though the bush was engulfed in flames, it didn't burn up" (Exod. 3:1–3, NLT).

Here God uses a common bush to get Moses' attention in a very uncommon way. God sets the bush on fire. Bushes caught fire in the desert all the time, but the uncommon thing was that this bush would not burn up.

So this is not a routine encounter with God. When God sees Moses come to investigate the burning bush, God calls his name twice to emphatically get his attention. Second chances are usually like this. God desires to do something personal and significant with and through our lives. It is often tied to some personal aspect of our lives—a failure or perhaps a mistake. Like Moses, we recognize it and cannot get away from it. In truth, God's connection with us must be this way and for this good reason.

Second chances are often defined by a bold challenge on God's part. This was certainly true for Moses. God's desire to connect with Moses was not to have small talk or pass the time of day. God called Moses to revisit some painful parts of his past. Then God said, "Now go, for I am sending you to Pharaoh. You must lead my people Israel out of Egypt" (Exod. 3:10, NLT).

Moses' heart must have pounded at the challenge placed before him. He had to have been overwhelmed in the moment. Please remember, Moses is an old man at this point in time. He has been in exile for 40 years, separated from his people and his family as the result of poor decisions. This often is the case. He probably hoped to be able to return one day, but certainly not as the liberator and deliverer of his people.

Moses was once the prince of Egypt and now is a fugitive from Egypt. Certainly, his days of hope were past, his bridge of return had been burned, and his dreams long since surrendered. Many of us feel the same way today as we look back over our mistakes and moral failures of the past.

Yet God's belief in Moses' life was still active and his plan for Moses was centered around action that would move Moses out of his comfort zone. Second chances are like that. They are usually tied to a challenge that will call for some uncomfortable action on our part. Think about some potential second chances that could be in your future. Won't they involve some uncomfortable action on your part? God may be calling you to...

- Restore a relationship that's been broken for many years
- Pursue a vocation change in the middle years of your life
- Forgive a person that you believe has wronged you
- Move past a failure and pursue new success in your life

Second chances are never sugar-coated, neatly wrapped, or as easy as A, B, C. No, most times second chances are defined by a radical life change. God calls us to life transformation and life reconstruction in some very personal way. These changes are anything but routine, so we feel a little overwhelmed when we first receive God's call. That is why:

Second chances require us to overcome our initial excuses. Notice in Exodus 3 and 4 that Moses responded to God's call in typical fashion. He made excuses:

- **I'm not that spiritual.** "Moses said to God, "Suppose I go to the Israelites and say to them, 'The God of your fathers has sent me to you,' and they ask me, 'What is his name?' Then what shall I tell them?" (Exod. 3:13, NLT).
- **What will people say or think?** "Moses answered, "What if they do not believe me or listen to me and say, 'The Lord did not appear to you'?" (Exod. 4:1, NLT).
- **I'm not gifted enough.** "Moses said to the Lord, 'Pardon your servant, Lord. I have never been eloquent, neither in the past nor since you have spoken to your servant. I am slow of speech and tongue'" (Exod. 4:10, NLT).
- **I simply can't do it.** "But Moses said, "Pardon your servant, Lord. Please send someone else" (Exod. 4:13, NLT).

In so many ways, we are like Moses. When God calls us to undertake a major task, we immediately begin to make excuses and explain to God why it will never work or why we shouldn't really have to do it. See if you can relate to any of these additional worn-out excuses:

It's too late.	**I'm too old.**	**That time has passed me by.**
They are the ones who started it.	**It wasn't my fault.**	**I did everything I could.**
Too much water has passed under that bridge.		**The ball is in their court.**
	They need to make the first move.	

Like Moses, the question for us is not, Will we get a second chance? The question is, Will we take advantage of a second chance? For most of us, that begins with overcoming easy excuses and responding to a bold challenge through action.

Second chances depend on action, perseverance, and the God Factor. From the very beginning, that was that true for Moses. Exodus 4:20 gives us these words: "So Moses took his wife and sons, put them on a donkey, and headed back to the land of Egypt" (NLT). Second chances are always dependent on taking an initial step. Luckily for us today, that does not normally require us to get a donkey! However, it does include perseverance as it did for Moses in crossing the Red Sea or praying for food in the wilderness. Those moments in his journey not only required perseverance but also needed the God Factor to be on hand. Those moments occur when obstacles come into view that are larger than our personal capacity to conquer and we need God to intervene.

That is the story of Genevie Kocourek, who fulfilled a lifelong dream of becoming a doctor at age 59. In 2000, Kocourek was shivering in a tent when she had an epiphany. Then an information technology director who led rock-climbing trips in her spare time, she had enrolled in a wilderness first-responder course to learn how to care for injured climbers. "It was 38 degrees and raining," she recalls, "and I was having the time of my life!" In high school, Kocourek had dreamed of becoming a doctor, until a guidance counselor insisted that it wasn't "appropriate" for a woman. Now her passion was reignited. When she learned that her employer was offering early retirement, she mulled "retiring" to a brand-new career.

She and her husband Terry agreed that she'd keep working to avoid total loss of income while squeezing in pre-med courses such as chemistry on her lunch break or at night. Absorbing so much new information felt "like drinking from a fire hose," Kocourek says. But by 2004, she'd retired from her IT job, taken out a loan, and enrolled as a freshman at the University of Wisconsin's medical school.

Because the campus was 90 minutes away, Kocourek lived in student housing for the first two years and came home only on weekends. Her 81-year-old mother, who had recently moved in, helped with the cooking. When the isolation and course load overwhelmed her, Kocourek called Terry for pep talks. Still, she nearly quit during her third-year rotations, when she worked two days at a stretch, with no time for exercise and little contact with friends and family. She stuck it out. And in 2011, after finishing her residency, she founded her own holistic medicine practice, which combines traditional medicine with alternative therapies like massage and acupuncture. Says Kocourek: "The process of getting here was exactly what it needed to be— humbling, exhausting and wondrous" (Font, 2016).

Those final three words define acting on a second chance in multiple ways. It's *humbling* in the sense that we recognize our deficiencies in what we have done or have not done in life up to that point. It's *exhausting* in the sense that second chances normally require us to invest extra work in accomplishing the bold goal set before us. Finally, second chances are *wondrous* in the sense that when we review our journey, we recognize the presence, power, and provision of God along the way.

It was this way for Moses. With every excuse he made and obstacle he encountered, Moses found that God countered by revealing the wondrous reality of Himself. When God made this initial promise to

Moses—"And God answered, "I will be with you" (Exod. 3:12, NLT)—God understood that the fulfillment of this bold challenge would not ultimately be determined by Moses' deficiencies or sufficiencies. It would depend on the courage, grace, forgiveness, humility, strength, provision, and presence of God at work within and around Moses. This is what can be called the God Factor at work.

> SECOND CHANCES DEPEND ON THE AMOUNT OF WORK
> WE ARE WILLING TO PUT INTO THE GOAL SET BEFORE US.

In Moses' case and in ours, fulfilling a divine challenge ultimately depends on the presence and power of God. In the face of all the struggles and concerns presented in the journey, Moses simply trudged ahead, dependent on God's promise, "I will be with you." As Moses and the Israelites progressed toward the ultimate goal, they came to understand that God's promise was enough.

Our world has seen so many examples of this. The story is told of a young boy who was handed some homemade butter by his mother. She said, "Now I want you to go out and sell this butter door-to-door. I want you to ask 50 cents per pound but if they won't give you 50 cents per pound, tell them you'll take 25 cents per pound."

"Yes, ma'am," the boy said, "I can do that."

He went down the street a little way and knocked on a door. A very gruff man came to the door and said, "What do you want?"

"Well, my mom sent me out to sell this butter and she said that I should ask 50 cents per pound," the boy explained. "She also said if you wouldn't buy it for 50 cents per pound, I could sell it to you for 25 cents per pound. Do you want any?"

The man looked at him and said, "Son, I'm going to teach you a lesson. I'm going to give you 25 cents per pound, but I want you to know that if you hadn't told me what your mother said, I would have given you 50 cents per pound. You don't need to tell everybody everything you know."

The little boy took the quarter and put it in his pocket. As he walked off the porch, he said, "I didn't tell you everything I know. I didn't tell you that my cat fell in the butter."

There are so many truths and half-truths associated with the transactions and relationships of life that we often have difficulty telling the difference. However, I can tell you this with full confidence: Second chances are never easy. They will humble you, challenge you, exhaust you, and in many ways break you of your dependency on yourself. In the midst of all those trials, God's promise always holds true: "I will be with you." That means you have the full power of God's capacity in your situation. As the apostle Paul wrote, "I can do everything through Christ, who gives me strength" (Phil. 4:13 NLT). Every time God offers you a second chance, He offers with it the wondrous reality of Himself.

Remember the opening story of this chapter, when my dad and I visited a family that needed a second chance? Fast forward a little over forty years to November 15, 2014, the day before my Dad's memorial service. People were lined out the door of the funeral home for hours, waiting to pay their respects to this man I lovingly called Habey.

I was standing by the entry when a couple came in and the husband said with tearful eyes, "You probably don't remember us, but we owe your dad a lot. He helped us in a difficult time. We just wanted you to know how much we appreciated and respected him."

I smiled and said, "I know exactly who you are, and you will never know how good it is to see you again." At that moment, my mind went back to the day Dad stood next to that gentleman and shared what he simply called "some business."

Those folks took advantage of the second chance Dad offered them. They went on to start their own company and did quite well. They were well-respected in the community and blessed many others along the way. I shook my head, amazed at my father's capacity to see good in others and do good for them. His words still rang in my ears: "Son, sometimes all people need is a second chance." Perhaps that is true in your life. You need only make the decision to receive it.

Discussion questions

1. Is there someone you know who deserves a second chance?
2. What part could you play in making that second chance possible?
3. Is there an area in your own life where a second chance is needed?
4. What are your top two excuses for why you haven't acted on it?
5. Can your excuses be conquered by the truth that if God offers this chance, then God will be present with it?

A Life that Mattered

The Power of Generosity

A MEANINGFUL INCIDENT TOOK PLACE SOON AFTER MY DAD PASSED AWAY. Alzheimer's disease had slowly depleted his mental capacities and finally took his life. A couple of months after his memorial service, my mom had a doctor's appointment. I happened to be in town and was able to drive her to the appointment. Afterwards, we made our way to McDonald's for one of Mom's favorite snacks, a cup of coffee and an ice cream cone. We were sitting in a booth near the back of the store, reminiscing about Dad and discussing what a void his loss meant for all of us, particularly my mom.

With great gentleness and respect, a very distinguished older black gentleman approached our booth and said, "Excuse me, but are you Mrs. Daniels?

Mom replied, "Yes, I am."

"Mrs. Everett Daniels?"

"Yes, Everett was my husband."

The man continued, "My name is Howard Jones (not his real name). I heard about your husband's passing and wanted to say how sorry I was. If you don't mind, I wonder if I could sit down for a minute and share a story about your husband."

We both encouraged him to do so.

"Years ago, when I was in my early twenties, I worked at Daniels Roofing Company for a couple or three years," he said. "As both of you know, things were a little different back then." He smiled a smile that only someone who had lived through those racial struggles could have understood. "For some reason, your husband liked me and saw something in me. To make a long story short, your husband suggested I should go to college. Then he made that possible by paying for my college education."

"He did?" Mom said incredulously.

"Yes, ma'am, he did. That didn't happen a lot back then. I just want you to know that today I am a doctor and so is my daughter. We now live in the Midwest and I am down here visiting family. I am sorry to interrupt your conversation, but I wanted you to know what your husband did for me. More importantly, I wanted you to know that your husband's life mattered."

We shared with him our deep appreciation for taking the time to share his story. With that, he got up and left the building. My mom and I sat there for a silent moment, tears streaming down our faces, reminded once again of what we had lost. However, we were also reminded of how blessed we had been to have had the presence of Habey. I don't know if I will ever see that gentleman again or if he will ever know how much his brief encounter blessed my mom and me. Perhaps he will read this book and recognizes that his words contributed to its subtitle.

"A life that mattered" certainly described Dad. As I look back over the experiences I shared with him, I am reminded of how powerfully an ordinary person can use life to do good. Without fanfare or notoriety, he made a profound difference in the lives of others.

I do not think this happens by chance. It is a deliberate choice. If our lives are going to make a difference, we must come to understand this life principle: **We get out of life what we give to it and to others.** Winston Churchill said it this way: "We make a living by what we get; we make a life by what we give" (Cashman 2017, 123).

In Luke 6:38, Jesus said, "Give, and you will receive . . . The amount you give will determine the amount you get back" (NLT). The apostle Paul stated in 2 Corinthians 9:6, "Remember this: Whoever sows sparingly will also reap sparingly, and whoever sows generously will also reap generously." The truth is that every person has two ultimate choices in life: Will we live a life of generosity or one of selfishness?

Our answer to this question plays a huge part in determining the sphere of influence and the legacy we will have. Philanthropists like Warren Buffett and Bill and Melinda Gates have amassed multi-billion-dollar fortunes; but in the end they will be best known and admired for the work their foundations are doing to eradicate disease and offer better living conditions to hurting people around the world. Buffet and the Gates made an ultimate choice that their lives would have greater meaning if they used their means to strategically help others.

All of us face some critical decisions regarding a life of generosity. First, it is critical to determine that *we all have something to sow.*

Each person has a certain amount of seed to sow in this life. Some people have storehouses filled to abundance and some have storehouses almost bare. Yet even those with little have much compared to those who have nothing. What we must do is see all that we have as something that can be utilized to bless another.

Jack Kelley, foreign affairs editor for *USA Today* and nominated for a Pulitzer prize, tells this story:

> We were in Mogadishu, the capital of Somalia, in East Africa, during a famine. It was so bad we walked into one village and everybody was dead. There is a stench of death that gets into your hair, gets onto your skin, gets onto your clothes, and you can't wash it off.
>
> We saw this little boy. You could tell he had worms and was malnourished; his stomach was protruding. When a child is extremely malnourished, the hair turns a reddish color, and the skin becomes crinkled as though he's 100 years old.

Our photographer had a grapefruit, which he gave to the boy. The boy was so weak he didn't have the strength to hold the grapefruit, so we cut it in half and gave it to him. He picked it up, looked at us as if to say thanks, and began to walk back towards his village.

We walked behind him in a way that he couldn't see us. When he entered the village, there on the ground was a little boy who I thought was dead. His eyes were completely glazed over. It turned out that this was his younger brother.

The older brother kneeled next to his younger brother, bit off a piece of the grapefruit and chewed it. Then he opened up his younger brother's mouth, put the grapefruit in, and worked his brother's jaw up and down. We learned that the older brother had been doing that for the younger brother for two weeks. A couple of days later the older brother died of malnutrition and the younger brother lived. I remember driving home that night thinking, I wonder if this is what Jesus meant when He said, "There is no greater love than to lay down our life for somebody else" (Kelly 2000, 2).

There is not one person on earth who has nothing to offer. Whether it is our wisdom, skills, resources, or simply our time, we have something that can benefit another. However, the capacity to live a life that matters begins by determining that we will use whatever capacity life has bestowed on us to better and bless another.

It also important to determine *where we sow*. We need to sow in places that will bear the most fruit. Most large farmers today not only own land but lease land from others. The most successful farmers don't lease just any piece of land available. They lease land that they feel has the best opportunity to give them a generous harvest on what they sow. They are looking for the most fertile soil to sow their seed upon.

EACH OF US HAS SOMETHING THAT CAN BENEFIT ANOTHER.

In Matthew 13, Jesus describes a farmer sowing seed in different types of soil. Some soil was conducive to bearing a harvest and some was not. The intent of the parable is twofold. First, it encourages us to keep the soil of our hearts fertile to what God desires to grow in us. Second, it reminds us that not every soil we see or find ourselves in is the place we should invest ourselves.

When Ellen and I first moved into our house, our yard had all types of vegetation. The house had sat vacant for over two years and no care was given to the upkeep of the lawn. There were more weeds than grass and leftover concrete had been poured out in some areas of the yard. Some of the soil was rocky and packed down, and most of the yard had very little topsoil on it. So we went to work aerating and bringing in more topsoil for the barren and packed-down places. Over time, new growth began to take hold and the grass began to outgrow the weeds. But every year we had spots that would die and dry up in the heat of the summer. No matter what we tried; those sections seemed unable to get past the heat.

I asked a gentleman who worked for a landscaping company to stop by and give me an assessment of what was going on. He spent some time walking and digging around in the barren spots of the yard, then knocked on the door and asked me to join him outside. "I think I've found your problem," he stated. He then knelt down and began to dig through a section of the yard he noted had once been sodded. He said, "Your problem is that the dead stuff in those areas has never been removed; therefore, the water can't get through to nourish the new." Finally, he looked up at me and said, "Dead stuff is starving what needs to live."

Too many times that statement defines not only a difficult season of life but also the environment you are giving your life to. Is the soil of your life beaten down and packed down so hard that new life has difficulty finding root? Is the soil overridden with weeds and thistles to such a degree that it bears little harvest from your efforts? To say the least, it is not the fertile place that you hoped it would be, not a place that can yield a fitting harvest for your efforts.

The point is all of us have limited seed to sow and where we are sowing has a great impact on the productivity of the harvest we receive. In the parable of the sower, Jesus informs us that seed sown on fertile soil produced a crop that was thirty, sixty, and even a hundred times as much as had been planted (Matt. 13:23)! So we see that *where* we sow has a direct influence on the return of our efforts. Never underestimate the importance of where you sow your seed.

Third, it is critical to determine *how we sow*. Our generosity is not just determined by the reality that we have something to sow and that we have chosen where we sow. Another contributing factor is the attitude and intent of our planting. Some sow their seed with a closed fist and others with an open hand.

Most times, those who plant with a closed fist do so for control and power. These people give in order to manipulate a situation or control the actions of others. This is not just done with money, but with their affection, affirmation, and support. They are only willing to release blessings to others if it benefits themselves or rewards what they have predetermined as good or desired. It is not about what is good for the whole, but only for what they selfishly desire. When a person is described as "ruling with an iron fist," we mean they give with callous hearts and selfish intentions. This type person gives, not out of generosity, but out of a desire to hold power over others.

Other people sow with an open hand. For them, giving is not a means of control, but a means for blessing and benefitting others. This doesn't mean they are unwise and careless with their giving; however, they give for completely different reasons than to control or manipulate. Their greatest desire is to bless and lift up that which they love. They give in a way that allows others to determine how that resource is used and developed. They are not consumed with controlling or determining the ultimate outcome; instead, they trust others to work toward the good of the whole, just as they do.

I have a dear friend whose name is Ann Smith. She and her late husband, Nathan, were long-term missionaries to Japan before spending their senior years in Indiana. During those senior years they were anything but retired. Instead, they gave themselves to the training, encouragement, and support of younger leaders. After Nathan's passing, Anne has continued investing her life in the lives of others. Her goal is never to control or coerce others. Her only desire is to see young leaders soar higher than she did.

Please know, Ann and Nathan were not wealthy in a material sense; yet in every way possible they gave themselves, their home, their wisdom, their support, their love, their limited finances, and their experiences to others. Like Ann and Nathan, the beauty of sowing with an open hand is that we have so many ways to be generous. We do so with an understanding that God has blessed us to bless others.

Ann and Nathan's ultimate goal was to help others outgrow them and effect positive change. They poured themselves into others with an open-handed approach because they believed the greater outcome lay beyond themselves and their desires. They are the perfect examples that sowing with an open hand and sowing on fertile soil yields a harvest thirty, sixty, and even a hundred times as much as had been planted.

At its core, the gospel is the story of Jesus as the open hands of God. God gave without reservation in order that we might receive redemption in our lost and broken state. John 3:16 says, "For this is how God loved the world: He gave his one and only Son, so that everyone who believes in him will not perish but have eternal life" (NLT).

In other words, John says that God is our best example of giving. Through his Son, Jesus, God gave His all and His best. God gave sacrificially so that we might not only receive God's generosity but have an example of what generous giving looks like. As believers, we give in response to the open hands of God. In response to God's great generosity, we are called to give and live generously. Our role is to replicate the open hands of God by giving to provide good to others.

Mark and Kathy Fulton model that lifestyle for me. While attending Indiana University, Mark and Kathy began dating when participating in a musical variety show. After the completion of their undergraduate degrees, they married and have been together for more than thirty years. They have three adult children, a daughter-in-law, and three beautiful grandchildren.

During the early years of his dental practice, Mark served on a medical missions committee. Through this group, Mark and Kathy first participated on a weeklong mission trip to Haiti, where some basic dentistry was desperately needed. Mark and Kathy grew to love the people of Haiti and knew that the trip was just the first step of an adventure that would shape their future.

Through the years, the Fultons worked with other missionaries and mission organizations to establish a medical clinic in the village of St. Ard, Haiti. In 2005, the 8,000-square-foot clinic officially opened and now employs twenty indigenous personnel who provide medical, dental, and basic care to the underserved population in that area. As the clinic was being developed, the Fultons realized that they needed assistance in the management of the clinic, as well as financial accountability for the ministry. In response to these needs, they began Mission Haiti Medical, Inc., as a nonprofit organization to come alongside the ministry work.

The time needed to manage the clinic continued to grow as additional services were constantly being added. Mark and Kathy's work in Haiti continued to grow stronger as the demands of the clinic became greater and greater. Finally, in 2015, Mark and Kathy sold their well-established and very successful dental practice in the United States and moved to Haiti to oversee the growing ministry.

The Fultons are a great example of the open hands of God. Notice the progression of generous lives being formed. First, they recognized they had seeds of generosity to be sown. Their seed was medical and administrative giftedness that could make a profound difference in a Third World country. Second, their multiple trips established relationships that enabled them to identify most fertile place to sow that seed, Haiti. Finally, they determined that to have the greatest impact in Haiti, they would need to move there to sow with every component of their lives. They live and lead without any sense of power or position as their motivation. They work as partners with other ministry teams and only desire that the greater good will result from their efforts.

The Fultons illustrate so clearly for us that the harvest from our lives is directly tied to where we sow and how we sow. They understand that ultimately the condition of the soil and God's touch will determine the outcome of the harvest. Yet their first choice is to live a life of generosity as they bless others with the blessings God has given them.

Our second ultimate choice is this: Will we live a life of gratitude or one marked by bitterness? First Thessalonians 5:18 says, "Be thankful in all circumstances, for this is God's will for you who belong to Christ Jesus" (NLT).

Al Ells is one of the most gifted mentors I have ever known. His capacity to look deep inside a person by asking simple yet life-shaping questions is remarkable. Every opportunity Ellen and I spend time with him, we walk away very grateful that God saw fit to place Al in our lives. Al is the founder of Leaders that Last, a ministry that invests in leaders to enable them to have longevity and effectiveness in leadership and in life.

In that ministry's March 2016 newsletter, we read Al's article about overcoming the struggles of life through hope. Al began that article with the opening words of psychiatrist Scott Peck's book, *The Road Less Traveled*:

"Life is Difficult. This is a great truth, one of the greatest."

Al says that statement reminds us that no person leads an uncontested life of great joy, contentment, and peace. Unwanted storms batter each person's life. Even so, some individuals are able to rise above the adversity and make lemonade out of lemons.

All of us know people who face horrible tragedy and loss, yet they not only find a place of peace and resolution, but help others in the process. Al asks the questions:

What makes the difference between those who seem
to have thrived after adversity and those who don't?
Why do some people get better and others worse?

One of the answers—finding hope in the middle of the storm. When everything around us is being tested and life looks bleak, can we still have hope for a bright future? Can we believe that this tribulation will come to an end and that we will not be the worse for it; possibly even better for having endured? This is the battle for hope. It must be won if we are to overcome the difficulties of life and thrive anew. Hope is the salve that calms the pain and promotes new growth (Ells 2016, 1–3).

I am a firm believer that at the core of hope is gratitude. Grateful people have the unique capacity to find good where they are and to see the potential of where they are going. Grateful people certainly have difficult times, but choose not to linger in the abyss of misery. The attitude of gratitude causes them to look up instead of focusing down. Gratitude enables them to recognize there is good, even when the journey is not perfect.

In short, we must remember everyone experiences bitterness and brokenness. As Proverbs 14:10 says, "Each heart knows its own bitterness" (NLT).

Maxie Dunham informs us that bitterness "is a place on the life map for each of us" (Dunham 1987, 183) Yes, bitterness and brokenness come to all of us, and both can be experienced in varying degrees. Each can be experienced as a sideswipe or as a head-on collision. A sideswipe is a minor inconvenience, as when a trip we had planned gets canceled, a friend moves away, or perhaps a promotion falls through. With each of these, after some time has passed, life pretty much goes back to normal.

However, sometimes we experience something that feels more like a head-on collision. A spouse or child passes away, divorce tears apart a family, a parent chooses to be absent, a serious illness takes us captive, or another tragedy overtakes us in some way. When these types of events take place, life as we have known it is changed forever. Our gratitude could easily be overtaken by our bitterness.

Jim Hawkins was given that choice. Jim had joined the Marines at age 17 and was part of the many divisions that landed on the beachhead of Iwo Jima in World War II. During the landing and securing of that beach the Allied Forces suffered 26,000 casualties, with nearly 7,000 dead. As I grew to know Jim, he would share endless stories of his time in the military; but I will never forget one day when he paused and said, "Some experiences and some moments in your life, like Iwo Jima, change your life forever."

Later in his service to our country, Jim was wounded in Korea after being shot four times. He spent 22 months in the hospital recovering from those wounds. Still today, his diet is restricted, and he suffers from abdominal discomfort as a result of his injuries. Because of his bravery, Jim received the Silver Star, the Bronze Star, the Distinguished Medal of Honor and two Purple Hearts. Jim Hawkins was truly a living hero.

Like Jim Hawkins, we all have moments in life that bring great brokenness into our lives. After those difficult moments, the future trajectory of our lives will be determined by how we respond to the following question: Can we experience bitterness without becoming bitter?

In a survey done by *Discipleship Journal*, anger and bitterness were listed by believers as one of the top five spiritual challenges they face during their journey through life (Eisenman, 1992, 36–38). It is important to realize that as we brush up against bitterness, it has the potential to take root inside us. Bitterness can then spread its tentacles to all areas of a person's life. It is like going to an Italian restaurant and smelling like garlic when you leave. The smell of garlic not only clings to a person's clothes but makes its way into the pores of that person's skin. Bitterness, if clung to long enough, begins to define who a person is.

In the book of Ruth, Naomi is a perfect example of this. She and her husband, Elimelech, left their homeland of Judah and moved to Moab in hopes of finding a better life. Within ten years, Naomi had lost her husband and both sons. Talk about a head-on crash with bitterness! Soon after that, Naomi and Ruth, her daughter-in-law, returned to Bethlehem. When her friends heard she had returned, they all ran out to meet her, "Naomi, Naomi, how good it is to have you home. Welcome back!"

"Don't call me Naomi," she responded. "Instead call me Mara (Bitter), for the Almighty has made life very bitter for me. I went away full, but the LORD has brought me home empty. Why call me Naomi (which means Pleasant) when the LORD has caused me to suffer and the Almighty has sent such tragedy upon me?" (NLT) Naomi smells and talks like bitterness, don't you think?

Like Naomi, all of us will find ourselves at the pool of bitterness. It is not a question of if, but when. Then each of us will have a critical question to answer: Can we experience bitterness without becoming bitter?

For too many years after returning home from the war, Jim Hawkins was a bitter and angry man. The wounds and scars of his war-torn experiences were too great to leave behind and overcome. He thought relief was to be found in the booze he drank, and his emotional release was an anger so intense that damage always followed. No one could escape it. More times than not, his family became the target of his anger.

His intense brokenness continued for decades until, at age 67, Jim Hawkins met a man who changed him. The man's name was Jesus. Jim's life was so radically transformed by that relationship that some weeks and months later, his wife and children met this Jesus also.

I sat in amazement as Jim shared example after example of how this new relationship with God had transformed him and so many of his broken relationships. He described how the bitterness and anger had been overcome by the grace and mercy he had received from Jesus. So great was this transformation that at age 83, Jim went through the ordination process and became a pastor. He served in that capacity in an effort to share with others the healing he received from his incredible step of faith until his death a year ago.

As Jim stepped away from the pool of bitterness into the grace and forgiveness that Jesus offered him, his anger was replaced by the joy of knowing that his past was in the past. It did not need to define his present any longer. His bitterness was replaced with a sense of deep gratitude for what Jesus had done for him on the Cross. Redemption, restoration, and renewal swept over Jim as he accepted his new found faith. The heaviness of a broken and bitter past was lifted, and Jim Hawkins was made new. Jim experienced what Kinnaman and Lyons define as a central teaching of Jesus:

> Jesus taught that renewal—redemption, restoration, re-creation—is God's purpose for every human life. Pain, brokenness, and suffering are not to be avoided; they are to be endured because God redeems those experiences in order to renew and bless us (Kinnaman and Lyons 2016, 63).

Deep gratitude comes to those who understand and experience personal redemption. It is a gratitude that not only allows us to endure and move beyond brokenness and bitterness; it is so deep and meaningful that it shapes our lives and the legacy we leave behind. This wonderful process is a cornerstone to living a life that matters.

When we have deep gratitude for what has been given us and made possible for us, we understand our responsibility to share our blessings with others. What has been given us is not ours to hoard, but ours to steward. Out of the good given to us, we desire to do good others as a means of showing God our thanks for his grace and goodness to us.

It is my prayer that many of us can do this. I pray we can experience bitterness without becoming bitter and we can grow and learn gratitude and generosity, even when brokenness pierces our lives. I pray we will live lies of generosity rather than being guided by selfishness. Every life we touch is simply a "thank you" to God for touching, changing, redeeming, re-creating, and renewing us. When God's redemption and forgiveness are understood—I mean *really understood* and internalized—they call us to live in a grateful and generous manner. They call us to lead lives that matter and to become legacy makers.

Discussion questions

1. Up to this point, would your life be defined by generosity or selfishness, gratitude or bitterness?
2. How and where do you sow the blessings of your life?
3. In your brushes with brokenness, how have you grown and what have you learned?
4. How have those things enabled you to live a life that matters?

Conclusion
The Blessing of Closure

THE FORMER CHAPTER WAS IN SOME WAYS A CENTRAL PART OF MY FATHER'S story. Dad had his own struggles and hurts. His relationship to his own father was not always the most positive. Circumstances later in Dad's life caused division and hurt in that relationship. When my grandfather passed, I remember that my dad did not cry. I asked my mom why he didn't, and she simply replied to my six-year-old self, "Sometimes the hurt of the past is not easy to get over." It was much later in my life when I questioned Mom about that and she explained the brokenness my dad felt.

For a time in his late thirties, Dad struggled with depression. When I was a child, Dad would come home from work around 5:30 and go to bed around 6:30; the burden just too heavy to endure any more that day. During that time, the doctor suggested my dad take up a hobby to relieve some of the stress, so Dad decided to try golf.

On one of his first attempts, I went with him to caddy, even though I wasn't big enough to carry his golf bag. On the first tee, Dad's shot went astray and hit a bench where two women were seated. They dived away to safety.

In the aftermath, my father looked at me and said, "Roll, why don't you go and see if you can find that ball?" I may have only been 10 or 11, but I certainly knew better than to go down where those two women were getting up off the ground. I replied, "I don't think so."

Dad said, "Me either." So we waved at the two women as Dad yelled, "I'm sorry." We walked about 50 yards farther; where Dad dropped a ball in the fairway and played on.

As mentioned previously, Dad's redemption story began later in life and the lifestyle change dramatic. Simply put, faith changed my dad's life. In every way, his gratitude and generosity were lived out in remarkable ways. I never heard my dad speak critically of another person; I never heard him tell a lie; I never saw him lose his temper; and I never saw him treat Mom disrespectfully. At every turn, my dad's life was guided by gratitude and generosity. I close this book with a story about Dad that took place only a few short weeks before he died. I think it reflects the epitome of those life traits.

I was visiting my dad in the Alzheimer's care facility where he spent the closing season of his life. Hygiene was no longer a priority for him. This man who was always impeccably dressed and well-groomed now could not comprehend the daily requirements of keeping oneself properly clean and cared for.

Obviously, he had not shaved for several days and his hair needed trimming. During these last days, Dad avoided a shower like an eight-year-old boy does after playing in the yard. However, when I asked if he would like me to help him shower and shave, he said that would be fine.

In his latter few years, each family member had assisted with this routine many times. We walked into the bathroom and began reminding Dad of every step of each procedure. We could not simply say, "Go ahead and shower." We would put him in the shower and he would stand in the water for 15 seconds, forget why he was in there, and insist that it was time to get out. Therefore, each step of the process necessitated giving Dad detailed instructions while he constantly asked, "Why?" That question was repeated approximately thirty times for each task. But on this day, something was different. There was no struggle or questioning. He was like a little boy trusting his parent to do the things necessary to help him.

After the first 15 to 20 minutes, I began to see my dad again as the man I had known years before. If you have watched a loved one deteriorate with Alzheimer's, you are fully aware that after a time you begin to see just a shell of the person you used to know. In fact, the grief of losing your loved one to death begins years before they actually pass. At the end, you have been through such a prolonged journey of loss that you simply miss the person they once were and try to show respect for the shell of the person that remains. Memories will flood your mind about the person you are with, but they often can't even remember your name. You finally surrender to the fact that they can't comprehend the situation. You also recognize that their memories, like the persons they used to be, are now in a vault that was time-locked long ago.

However, this day was not like that. The father I once knew had somehow reappeared and wove himself into our conversation. A lucid moment would pass between us as he called me by name or spoke about my brother and sister in a current tense. I realized that this day was a privilege that I might never experience again. As I helped him towel off and put on his underclothes, I saw this incredibly bright and gracious man who had not only given me life, but had poured his life into me.

I took nothing for granted that day. I tried my very best to take in each precious moment as I combed his hair the way I had seen him meticulously do while I stood beside him as a young boy. I lathered his face and began to shave it; placing two fingers beside his sideburns before I shaved the whiskers below them. As I began shaving around his mouth and below his nose, he pursed his lips in the exact same way he always had when he was in control of the razor. Then I took scissors and began to trim the unruly hairs that grew in odd places. We laughed as I joked about weaving a blanket from the surplus hair his body had manufactured.

When we were done, I took a warm washcloth and gently rubbed his face clean. I took a hand towel, dried his face, and applied the after-shave lotion that he had used since the beginning of time. Its fragrance took me back to my childhood when this man, my father, was strong and vibrant. It was then that the moment happened.

Dad turned around and faced me. Those steel-blue eyes that could look into your soul looked directly into mine. There was no cloudiness in that moment, no look of confusion. These were the eyes of my dad that danced when he laughed, pierced me when I needed a reprimand, uplifted me when he said he was proud of me, and challenged me when he shared his words of wisdom. Then he simply said, "Rol, I can't thank you enough for doing this. It means the world to me that you would take the time. I love you, son."

With that, he paused a moment, still looking into my eyes. We both seemed to know we would never share a moment like this again, but he was unafraid of the ending that was coming soon. I stood absolutely still, praying, hoping that moment would last forever. I dared not let even a breath interrupt what I could never get back. Then Dad turned and looked back into the mirror. The moment was gone, like so many others.

I wept and pulled him close, hugging him tightly. I prayed he could feel the deep love and admiration I had for him. I so wanted him to sense how thankful I was to have him as my father. Every beat of my heart cried out from the grief of losing the rock this man had been in my life and in my family's life. So I held him as he stood within the folds of my arms. That day would be the last time I would see Dad alive. It was the last living moment I shared with him, and I cannot thank God enough for the preciousness of it. It was a gift of closure that I will cherish the rest of my life.

As I drove away from the extended-care facility, I thought about Dad's last words to me and I laughed. It occurred to me that Dad had spoken words of gratitude. He was grateful to the end for even the simplest of gestures when his life was so muddied by fear and confusion. I have no doubt that my father's life made such a powerful difference because the attributes of generosity and gratitude defined him. He never hoarded the blessings God had given him. He simply saw his blessings as something to share, a way to bless and bring good to others.

His gratitude went deeper than a simple "thank you" for the stuff he had. It began when the redeeming power of Jesus changed his life, when his past was overwhelmed by the new beginning he found in Christ's grace. The struggle to measure up was replaced by an unconditional love so great that he knew he was loved simply for who he was. My dad began a new life at forty when he was redeemed, restored, and recreated from the brokenness and hurt of everything in the past.

It is the kind of life I hope you will come to understand and dare to take hold of—a life guided by these simple principles. Each of us has the opportunity to make a profound difference in other people's lives by simply taking hold of generosity, gratitude, and selflessness. At their core, each principle shared in this book is tied to these characteristics that the Cross of Jesus made possible.

The selfless love of Jesus is the foundational premise on which Kinnaman and Lyons wrote. They remind us that if we do good works "for the sake of our own reputation, to make ourselves look good, to generate positive publicity, or to make people like us more, we are getting good wrong. Our good works should cause others to praise the Father, not us. If we are trying to do good works to make ourselves worthy of God's love, we are getting good wrong. Our good works should be a response of selfless love toward others in thanks for Jesus's unconditional love for us" (Kinnaman and Lyons 2016, 71–72).

They got it right. My father got it right. If we live unselfishly, then we can get it right also. My hope and prayer is that you begin today living to create a lasting legacy because that is life at its best. Habey certainly thought so and certainly lived that way. It is my hope that we also live a life that matters.

A Letter to My Sons

To my wonderful sons, Tyler and Seth,

I wrote *Legacy Maker* for you. Honestly, this was not an arduous process but a true labor of love. As I pondered this incredible man we called Pops, I was reminded of how proud he was of the two of you and how much he loved being a part of your lives.

At its core, this book was written with the hope that both of you catch a better glimpse of what made your grandfather the man he was. Dad was not one to broadcast his beliefs to others; but his consistent lifestyle brought to light what he believed. Over the years, I watched him care for and give to others with no notice or recognition of what he was doing. His constant example instilled in me the reality that resources are best used to bless others and faith is better displayed than only talked about. The principles and values that are in this book are the ones he lived out constantly and without compromise.

Your granddad was a man who loved to laugh and did so often. A man who carried himself with dignity and always treated others that way. A man who worked hard but knew how to play with those he loved and cared for. A man whose word was his bond and honesty was his trademark. A man who was given to his faith and never wavered from that walk. A man who loved his wife and children with intensity and passion until the end. And a man who gave much more than he ever took and left this world a much better place.

As I have grown older, I've recognized the blessing of having significant people shape one's life. As you know, Pops certainly did that for me in many different areas and ways. I trust this book will enable him to do the same in your lives, as well. Please know, I see great evidence of that already and could not be more proud of you in any shape, form or fashion. Tyler and Seth, I already consider my life to be a success because of the men you have grown to be. This book is for you and so is the love with which it was written.

All my love,
Dad

References

Anderson, A. R. "Decide in Advance to Do the Right Thing." *Forbes/ Entreprenuers*, Dec 6, 2012, 1-3. Retrieved January 20, 2016 from http://www.forbes.com/sites/amyanderson/2012/12/06/decide-in-advance-to-do-the-right-thing/#2715e4857a0b2246cd0c232d

Barnum, Thaddeus. *Real Identity: Where Bible and Life Meet*. Indianapolis, IN: Wesleyan Publishing House, 2013.

Bombeck, E. Erma. *Bombeck Quotes*. BrainyQuote.com, Brainy Media Inc., 2019. https://www.brainyquote.com/quotes/erma_bombeck_130034, accessed October 9, 2019.

Born Again. A Robert L. Munger production, Produced by Frank Capra Jr., AVCO Embassy Pictures, 1978.

Boyum, G. *The Historical and Philosophical Influences on Greenleaf's Concept of Servant Leadership: Setting the Stage for Theory Building*. Paper presented at the Academy of Human Resource Development International Research Conference in the Americas, Panama City, FL, February 2008.

Burns, R. *Poems, chiefly in the Scottish dialect*. Kilmarnock: John Wilson, 1786, 138.

Cashman, K. *Leadership from the Inside Out: A Leader for Life*. Oakland, CA: Berrett-Koehler Publishing, Inc., 2017.

Chambers, O. *My Utmost for His Highest*. Uhrichsville, OH: Barbour Publishing, Inc., 1935.

Chickering, A. W., Dalton, J. C., & Stamm, L. *Encouraging Authenticity & Spirituality in Higher Education*. San Francisco: Jossey-Bass, 2006.

Churchill, William S. *Never Give In! The Best of Winston Churchill's Speeches.* New York, Hyperion, 2003.

Cloud, H. *Integrity: The Courage to Meet the Demands of Reality.* New York: HarperCollins Publishers, 2006.

Collins, J. *Good to Great: Why Some Companies Make the Leap . . . and Others Don't.* New York, NY: HarperCollins Publishers, Inc., 2001.

Covey, S. *Seven Habits of Highly Effective People.* New York: Simon and Schuster, 2004. *Principled-centered leadership.* New York: Fireside, 1990.

Merrill, A. R., & Merrill, R. R. *First Things First.* New York: Simon and Schuster, 1995.

Doer, J. *Measure What Matters: How Google, Bono, and the Gates Foundation Rock the World with OKRs.* New York, Penguin Random House, LLC, 2018.

Dunnam, M. *The Communicator's Commentary: Exodus.* Ogilvie, L. general editor. Waco, TX: Word Books Publisher, 1973.

Eldridge, J. *Wild at Heart: Discovering the Secret of a Man's Soul.* Nashville, TN: Thomas Nelson, Inc., 2010.

Ells, Al. The battle for hope. Mesa, AZ: "Leaders That Last." *The Emerging Leader Newsletter, 1-3,* March 2016. Retrieved April 16, 2016, http://www.leadersthatlast.org

Eisenman, Tom. "Fighting to Win." Discipleship Journal. November/December, 1992, 36-38.

Engberg, M. E. "Educating the Workforce for the 21st Century: A Cross-Disciplinary Analysis of the Impact of the Undergraduate Experience on Student Development of a Pluralistic Orientation." *Research in Higher Education,* 48:2007.

Font, R. "The 'Humbling, Exhausting, Wondrous' Experience of Becoming a Doctor at 59." Retrieved February 11, 2016, http://www.oprah.com/spirit/Second-Chances-in-Life#ixzz3zsZjEkXA

Greenleaf, R. K. *The servant as leader.* Indianapolis, IN: The Robert K. Greenleaf Center, 1991.

Hoosiers, written by Angelo Pizzo and directed by David Anspaugh, produced by Hemdale Film Corporation, Los Angeles, CA. Released 1986.

Johnson, F. *Keeping Faith: A Skeptic's Journey*. New York, Houghton Mifflin Company, 2003.

Jones, B. "Do the Right Thing." The Random Acts of Kindness Foundation. Retrieved January 20, 2016 from https://www.randomactsofkindness.org/the-kindness-blog/2868-always-do-the-right-thing

Kelly, J. "Stories behind the Headlines." Speech given at Evangelical Press Association convention in May 2000. Retrieved March 22, 2016 @ at http://www.sermoncentral.com/sermons/your-big-brother-jesus-charles-salmon-sermon-on-humanity-of-christ-71061.asp?Page=3

Kennedy, J. "Message from an Empty Tomb." *Preaching Today*, 1999: 66.

King, S. "What You Pass on." *Family Circle Magazine*, November 1, 2001, 156. Retrieved March 22, 2016 from http://www.epm.org/static/uploads/downloads/stephen-king-giving-ahndout.pdf

Kinnaman, D. & Lyons, G. *Good Faith: Being a Christian When Society Thinks You're Irrelevant and Extreme*. Grand Rapids, MI: Baker Books, 2016.

Kouzes, J. M. & Posner, B. Z. *A Leader's Legacy*. San Francisco, CA: Jossey-Bass, 2006.

Leider, R. *The Power of Purpose: Find Meaning, Live Longer, Better*. San Francisco, CA: Berrett-Koehler Publishers, 2010.

Miller, D. 2019. "Fatigue Makes Cowards of Us All." https://www.48days.com › fatigue-makes-cowards-of-us-all. Retrieved June 17, 2019.

Munger, R. *My Heart, Christ's Home*. Downers Grove, IL: InterVarsity Press, 1986.

Murray, A. *Abide in Christ*. New Kensington, PA: Whitaker House, 1979.

Parrott, L. *3 Seconds: The Power of Thinking Twice*. Grand Rapids, MI: Zondervan, 2007.

Peck, A. S. *The Road Less Traveled: A New Psychology of Love, Traditional Values and Spiritual Growth*. New York, NY: Simon and Schuster, Inc., 1978.

Phuc, K. "These Bombs Led Me to Christ." *Christianity today,* May 2018, 88. Retrieved January 19, 2019. https://www.christianitytoday. com/ct/.../napalm-girl-kim-phuc-phan-thi-fire-road.html

Scazzero, P. *The Emotionally Healthy Church.* Grand Rapids, MI: Zondervan Publishing House, 2010.

Seamands, D. *Healing for Damaged Emotions.* Colorado Springs, CO: David C. Cook Publishing, 1981.

The Bucket List, directed by Rob Reiner, screenplay written by Justin Zackham, produced by Rob Reiner, Craig Zadan, Neil Meron, Alan Griesman, Warner Bros. Inc., Burbank, CA: released 2007.

Waitley, Dennis. "Your Absolute Bottom Line," *Priorities*, 2003, 26.

Ward, L. "The Path to Purpose," September 25, 2015. Retrieved November 4, 2015 from http://www.livehappy.com/practice/ path-purpose

Warren, R. *The Purpose Driven Life: What on Earth Am I Here For?* Grand Rapids, MI: Zondervan Publishing House, 2002.

Welch, R. *We Really Do Need Each Other.* Grand Rapids, MI: Zondervan Publishing House, 1982.

Wellman, S. *Gladys Aylward: Missionary to China (Heroes of the Faith).* Uhrichsville, OH: Barbour Publishing, Inc., 1998.

Wilson, T. "What Matters Most." *Exponential Ministries*, 2018 blog review. Retrieved June 13, 2018 http://www.outreachmagazine. com/features/leadership/30274-measure-what-matters.html

Yukl, G. *Leadership in Organizations,* 5th ed. Upper Saddle River, NJ: Prentice Hall, 2002.

Zandy, A. "If You Want to Lead...Learn to Serve." *Debt Cubed*, 2007:22, 24–25.

Printed in the United States
By Bookmasters